THE ETHICS OF ARISTOTLE

VOLUME THE SECOND

Revised from the Translation by D. P. Chase
published at Oxford in 1847

ARISTOTLE

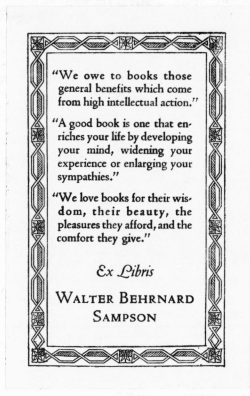

LONDON:
ARTHUR L. HUMPHREYS
1902

ARISTOTLE

BOOK VI

CHAPTER I

E have already said that it is right to choose the mean and not the excess or defect, and that the mean is what right reason prescribes; let us now proceed to explain this term.

For in all the moral habits which we have expressly mentioned, as well as in all others, there is, so to speak, a certain mark which the rational man keeps in view in increasing or relaxing his efforts, and there is a certain limit of those mean states which we say are in accordance with right reason, and lie between excess on the one hand, and defect on the other.

Now to speak thus is true enough, but conveys no very definite meaning: as, in fact,

II. A

in all other pursuits requiring attention and diligence, on which skill and science are brought to bear, it is quite true of course to say that men are neither to labour nor relax too much or too little, but in moderation, and as right reason directs; yet if this were all a man were told, he would not be greatly the wiser; as, for instance, if in answer to the question, what sort of remedies ought to be applied to the body, he were to be told to apply whatever remedies the science of medicine orders, and in such manner as the physician directs.

And so in the case of the mental states, it is not only requisite that the rule we have laid down should be true, but further, that it should be determined what right reason is, and what is the definition of it.

**THIS IS THE END OF THE
FIRST CHAPTER**

CHAPTER II

IN our division of the virtues of the soul, we said that some of them were moral and others intellectual. We have already discussed the moral virtues, and we will now proceed to consider the others, after some preliminary remarks upon the soul itself. It was stated before, you will remember, that the soul consists of two parts, the rational and the irrational : we must now make a similar division of the rational part.

Let it be assumed, then, that there are two divisions of the rational part, one, that by which we contemplate those existences whose principles are invariable, and one, that by which we contemplate those existences whose principles are variable. For when things are generically different, there must be generically different parts of the soul which are naturally adapted to each of them, since these

3

parts of the soul possess their knowledge in virtue of a certain resemblance and affinity between themselves and the objects of which they are percipients. Let us call the former, the scientific, and the latter, the deliberative part. For deliberating and calculating are the same, and no one ever deliberates about such things as are invariable. The calculative then is one part of the rational part of the soul.

It remains to determine what is the perfect state of each of these two parts of the soul, for that will be the virtue of each. But its virtue will be relative to its proper function.

There are three faculties in the soul which influence moral action and truth, namely, sense, reason, and appetite or desire. Of these, sense cannot originate any moral action, as is seen from the fact that brutes have sense, but are incapable of moral action.

If we take the other faculties, we see that pursuit and avoidance in desire correspond to affirmation and negation in reason. And so since moral virtue is a state of deliberate moral choice or purpose, and moral purpose is

desire consequent on deliberation, the reason
must be true and the desire right, to constitute good moral purpose, and what the reason
affirms, the desire must pursue.

This kind of reasoning and this kind of
truth are concerned with moral action. But
truth and falsehood must be the good and
the bad of that reasoning which is purely
speculative, and concerned neither with action
nor production, because this is manifestly the
function of the intellect, while the function
of the practical intellect is the apprehension
of truth in agreement with right desire.

Moral purpose, then, is the origin of moral
action, that is, what actually sets it in motion,
not the final cause, and the origin of moral
purpose is desire, and reason directed to a
certain result, so that moral purpose implies
reason or intellect on the one hand and a certain moral state on the other: for right action
and wrong action are alike impossible without
both intellect and moral character.

But the mere intellect can never set anything going, but only when it is directed to
a certain end, that is, it must be practical.

For the practical intellect governs the productive, as every one who produces anything, produces with an object in view; and that which is or may be produced, is not an end in itself, but is relative to something else, and belongs to something: whereas action is an end in itself, the end of the action being nothing more than that it should be done well, and this is the object of desire. Moral purpose, then, may be defined as reason influenced by desire, or as desire qualified by reason; and it is this originative faculty which constitutes a man.

But nothing which is done and past can be an object of moral purpose; for instance, no man purposes to have sacked Troy; because, in fact, no one ever deliberates about what is past, but only about that which is to come, and which may therefore be influenced, whereas what is past cannot possibly be other than it is: and so Agathon is right in saying,

'Of this alone is Deity bereft,
    To make undone whatever hath been done.'

Thus then truth is the apprehension of function of both the intellectual parts of the soul; and consequently the virtue of each part will be that state which will best enable it to arrive at the truth.

THIS IS THE END OF THE SECOND CHAPTER

CHAPTER III

ET us discuss these virtues again, commencing again from the beginning. Let us assume that the means by which the soul arrives at truth in affirmation or negation are five in number, namely, art, science, prudence, wisdom, intuitive reason; for conception and opinion may lead to error.

What science is, is clear from the following considerations, if one is to speak accurately, instead of being led away by resemblances. We all conceive that what we scientifically know is invariable, but as to those things which are variable, we cannot say whether they are in existence or not, the moment they cease to be within the sphere of our actual observation.

So, then, the object of science is necessary, and therefore eternal; for all things that are necessary in themselves are eternal, and that which is eternal has neither beginning nor end.

Again, all science is thought to be capable of being taught, and that which is an object of science capable of being learned. But all teaching is based upon previous knowledge, as we have explained in the Analytics, for there are two ways of teaching, by syllogism or by induction. Now, induction is a principle, and leads up to universal principles, while syllogism starts from these universal principles. There are principles then, from which syllogism starts, which are not arrived at by syllogism, cannot be themselves proved, and which therefore must be arrived at by induction.

Science then may be defined as a habit or faculty of demonstration, with all the further qualifications, that we add to the definition in the Analytics. For a man, strictly and properly speaking, has scientific knowledge only when he has a certain kind of belief, and is sure of the principles on which his belief rests: as unless these principles are better known to him than the conclusions, such knowledge as he has will be merely accidental.

Let this then be accepted as our definition of science.

THIS IS THE END OF THE THIRD CHAPTER

CHAPTER IV

THAT which is variable includes the objects of production and action, but production is different to action. We may trust the popular view on this point. The habit or faculty of acting with reason, is different from the faculty of producing with reason; and so neither of them is included in the other, for action is not production, nor is production action. But as architecture is an art, and may be described as a certain faculty of producing with reason, and as there is no art which is not a faculty of this kind, nor any faculty of this kind which is not an art, it follows that an art, in its strict and proper sense, must be the same thing, a faculty of producing with true reason.

Now all art has to do with production, that is, with contriving, and seeing how to produce some one of those things that can

11

either be or not be, and the cause of whose production rests with the producer and not with the thing produced.

For art is not concerned with things which exist or come into being of necessity, nor with the products of nature, for the original cause of these things lies in themselves. Production and action being different, art must be concerned with production, and not with action. And in a certain sense art and fortune are concerned with the same things, as Agathon says,

' Art Fortune loves, and is of her beloved.'

Art, then, as has been stated, is a certain faculty or habit of production with true reasoning or calculation; the absence of art, on the contrary, is the habit of production with false reasoning or calculation, and both are concerned with that which is variable.

THIS IS THE END OF THE FOURTH CHAPTER

CHAPTER V

E may ascertain the nature of prudence, by considering who they are whom we call prudent.

It seems to be characteristic of the prudent man to be able to deliberate well upon what is good or expedient for himself, not in any particular sense, as for example, the means to health or strength, but upon the means of living well. This view is confirmed by the fact that we sometimes apply the term 'prudent' to those who deliberate well in some particular line, when they calculate well with a view to some particular good end, and in matters that do not fall within the scope of art. And so, in a general way of speaking, the man who is good at deliberation will be prudent. But no man deliberates upon things which cannot be altered, or upon such as lie beyond the range of his own action. Now science implies demonstration, but things

13

whose principles are variable do not admit
of demonstration, for all the results of such
principles are variable; and, on the other
hand, such things as are necessary do not
admit of deliberation. It follows then that
prudence cannot be a science or an art; not
the former, because the sphere of action is
variable, not the latter, because action and
production are generically different.

It remains then that prudence must be
a faculty or habit of correct reasoning on
matters of action, and concerned with those
things which are good or bad for man; for
while production has another end than itself,
it is not so with action, as right action is in
itself an end.

For this reason we think that Pericles
and men like him were prudent men, because
they could see what was good for themselves
and for mankind in general, and we also
think those men are prudent who are skilled
in domestic management or civil government.
This, too, is the reason why we call temperance by the name which in Greek it bears,
etymologically signifying, 'that which preserves

prudence;' for temperance does preserve the right opinion of one's own true interest.

For it is not every kind of opinion that is destroyed or perverted by pleasure and pain, as, for instance, that the three angles of every rectilineal triangle are equal to two right angles, but only those opinions bearing on moral action.

For the principles of the matters of moral action are the final cause of them; but when a man has been corrupted by pleasure or pain, the principle immediately becomes obscured, and he no longer sees that it is his duty to choose and act in each instance with a view to this final cause, and by reason of it; for vice has a tendency to destroy the moral principle. Our conclusion, then, is that prudence must be a faculty or habit of correct reasoning on matters of action, and concerned with that which is good for man.

Then again art admits of degrees of excellence, but prudence does not; and in art voluntary error is preferable to involuntary, but not so in the case of prudence, or the other virtues. It is clear then prudence is a virtue or excellence of a certain kind, and not an art.

As there are two rational parts of the soul, prudence must be the virtue of that part, whose province is opinion, for both opinion and prudence are concerned with that which is variable. And further, prudence is something more than a habit of correct reasoning, as is proved by the fact that such a habit may be forgotten and so lost, while prudence cannot be so lost.

THIS IS THE END OF THE
FIFTH CHAPTER

CHAPTER VI

CIENCE is a mode of conceiving universal and necessary truths, but truths that can be demonstrated imply first principles, and since science is impossible without reasoning, every science has its principles.

It follows that the principles on which scientific truth depends cannot fall within the scope of science, or art, or prudence; for a scientific truth can be demonstrated, but art and prudence are concerned with that which is variable. Nor can they come within the scope of wisdom, for the wise man must in some cases depend on demonstrative reasoning.

Since then, the faculties whereby, without possibility of error, we always attain truth, when dealing with such things as are necessary or contingent, are science, prudence, wisdom, and intuition, and the faculty

which takes in first principles cannot be any
of the three first; the last, namely intuition,
must be the faculty which performs this
function.

THIS IS THE END OF THE
SIXTH CHAPTER

'ISDOM' is a term we use principally in two meanings: in the first place, in the arts we ascribe it to those who are the greatest masters of their art; to Phidias, for instance, as a sculptor; and to Polyclitus, as a statuary; meaning, in this instance, nothing else than excellence of art: in the other sense, we think some people to be wise in a general way, not in any particular line or in any particular thing, but as Homer says in the Margites; 'Him the Gods made neither a digger of the ground, nor ploughman, nor in any other way wise.'

It is plain, then, that wisdom, in this general sense, will be the most perfect of the sciences. But if this is so, then the wise man must not merely know the deductions from the first principles, but also know the truth about those principles. Wisdom therefore will be the union of intuition and science; it is, so to speak, science of the noblest objects, being as it were a head.

For it would be absurd to suppose that political science or prudence is the highest knowledge, unless man is the most excellent of all that exists in the universe. Now if the terms wholesome and good mean one thing when applied to men and another thing when applied to fishes, but the terms white and straight always have the same meaning, we must allow that the term wise has always the same meaning, while the term prudent has different meanings. For whatever is keenly attentive to its own interests is called prudent, and would be entrusted with the charge of those interests. And for this reason, we call some brutes prudent if they have a faculty of fore-thought respecting their own subsistence.

And it is quite plain that wisdom and statesmanship cannot be identical; for if we give the name of wisdom to knowledge of what is expedient for ourselves, there will be many kinds of wisdom: there will not even be one wisdom having regard to the good of all animals, but different for different animals: it can no more be one than the art of healing can be one and the same for all living beings.

If it is urged, that man is superior to all other animals, that makes no difference; for there are many other things more god-like in their nature than man, as, to take the most obvious instance, the elements of which the universe is composed.

It is plain then, that wisdom is the union of science and intuition, and has for its objects those things which are most noble in their nature. Accordingly, people call Anaxagoras, Thales, and men of that stamp, wise, but not prudent, seeing them to be ignorant of their own interests; and say, that their knowledge is something quite out of the common, wonderful, hard of attainment, and superhuman, but still useless, because they do not seek after what is good for them as men.

THIS IS THE END OF THE SEVENTH CHAPTER

CHAPTER VIII

RUDENCE, on the other hand, is concerned with human affairs, and with matters that admit of deliberation. For we say, to deliberate well is most peculiarly the function of the prudent man, and no man deliberates about what is invariable, or about matters which have no definite end, or whose end is not some realisable good. And, in the most general sense, he is said to deliberate well, who, by a process of reasoning or calculation, aims at that which is best for man in practical life.

Nor again does prudence consist in a knowledge of general principles only, but in addition to this a knowledge of particular details is necessary, for prudence is a practical virtue, and in practice we have to do with particulars. This is the reason why some men who have not much knowledge are more

practical than others who have, especially
men who possess actual experience; for if
a man knows that light meats are easy of
digestion, and wholesome, but does not know
what kinds of meat are light, he will not
cure people so well as a man who only knows
that the flesh of birds is light and wholesome.
But prudence is a practical virtue, so that
we ought to have the knowledge, both of
general principles, and of particular facts, but
especially the latter. So that here also there
will be a supreme form of prudence.

Again, statesmanship and prudence are
the same faculty, but the point of view is
not the same.

Of this faculty in its application to the
state, the supreme form is the faculty of legislation, but the subordinate form which is concerned with particular cases is called by the
generic name statesmanship, and its functions
are action and deliberation, for a decree, as
being the extreme, is itself the subject of
action. Therefore, those who exhibit this
form of prudence are alone said to be statesmen, for they alone act like handicraftsmen.

But prudence in the most proper sense is generally thought to refer to one's individual interests; and it is this form which usually receives the generic name of prudence: the other forms being called domestic economy, legislation, and statesmanship, which is subdivided into two branches, the deliberative and the judicial. Now it seems that knowing what is good for one's self is one kind of knowledge, though it admits of great variety; and it is a common idea, that the man who knows and busies himself about his own concerns merely, is prudent, while statesmen, are considered busybodies, as Euripides says, 'How foolish am I, who whereas I might have shared equally, idly numbered among the multitude of the army . . . for Jupiter hates them that are busy and meddlesome.' For men generally seek their own good, and hold that this is their proper business. It is then from this opinion that the notion arises, that such men are prudent. And yet it is perhaps possible, that the good of the individual cannot be secured, independently of connection with a family or a community.

And again, how a man should manage his own affairs is sometimes not quite plain, and needs consideration.

And this is confirmed by the fact that the young become geometricians, and mathematicians, and wise in such matters, but cannot possibly, it is thought, become prudent. The reason is, that prudence has for its object particular facts, which can only become known by experience. But it is impossible for a young man to be experienced, as experience is the fruit of years.

Why, again, it may be asked, can a boy become a mathematician, but not wise or a natural philosopher? And the answer surely is, that mathematics is an abstract science, but the principles of wisdom and natural philosophy are derived from experience, and thus young men do not believe, although they may repeat, propositions of the latter kind, but they easily comprehend the meaning of mathematical truths.

Again, error in deliberation may lie either in the universal or in the particular judgment: for instance, you may be wrong in judging that all water of a certain gravity is bad, or that some particular water is of that gravity.

But it is evident that prudence is not science, for prudence has to do with the extreme, as has been said, because every object of action is of this nature.

Prudence is opposed to intuition, for intuition deals with those principles which cannot be proved by reasoning, while prudence is concerned with ultimate particular facts which cannot be scientifically proved, but are perceived by sense; not one of the five special senses, but a sense analogous to that by which we perceive in mathematics that no rectilineal figure can be contained by less than three lines, that is, that the ultimate figure is a triangle, for here also our reasoning must come to a stop.

This faculty, however, is sense rather than prudence, for prudence cannot be thus defined.

**THIS IS THE END OF THE
EIGHTH CHAPTER**

CHAPTER IX

UT investigation and deliberation are not the same, for deliberation is a particular form of investigation. We ought to ascertain what good deliberation is, whether it is a kind of science, or opinion, or happy conjecture, or some other kind of faculty. It obviously is not science, for men do not investigate subjects which they know, but good deliberation is a kind of deliberation, and the man who deliberates, investigates and calculates.

Neither is it happy conjecture; for happy conjecture is an irrational and hasty operation; but men deliberate a long time, and it is a common saying, that one should execute speedily what has been resolved upon in deliberation, but deliberate slowly.

Sagacity, again, is different from good deliberation, for sagacity is a species of happy conjecture. Nor is good deliberation opinion of any kind.

Well, then, since he who deliberates ill, errs, while he who deliberates well, is said to deliberate rightly, it is clear that good deliberation is rightness of some kind, but not a rightness or correctness of science or of opinion; for science does not admit of correctness any more than of error, and correctness of opinion is truth; and, again, whatever is a matter of opinion is something already settled.

But yet, good deliberation is impossible without the exercise of reason. Does it remain then that it is correctness of reasoning simply, as reasoning does not amount to assertion? and whereas opinion is not investigation, but already a definite assertion, when we are deliberating, whether well or ill, we are engaged in investigation and calculation?

Well, good deliberation is a kind of correctness in deliberation, and so we must first inquire what is the nature and what the subjects of deliberation. Now, there are various kinds of correctness, and it is clear that it is not every kind of correctness in deliberation that constitutes good deliberation; for the incontinent, or bad man, will obtain from his deliberation the results which he desires; and so he may be said to have deliberated correctly in one sense, though what he has gained is a great evil. But to have deliberated well is thought to be a good thing, for good deliberation is only such correctness of deliberation as arrives at what is good.

But it is possible to arrive at what is good by false reasoning, that is, to arrive at what ought to be done, but not by right means, the middle term being false. And so this will not be a case of good deliberation, when one arrives at a right conclusion, but not by the right means.

Again, one man arrives at the right conclusion after long deliberation, another quickly. So that before described, will not yet be good deliberation, but good deliberation is that correctness of deliberation which arrives at a right conclusion, and arrives at it in the right manner and at the right time.

Lastly, a person may deliberate well, either generally, or towards some particular end. Good deliberation in a general sense is such as leads correctly to the general end. Good deliberation of a particular kind is such as leads correctly to a particular end. And so if it is characteristic of prudent men to deliberate well, good deliberation must be correctness in judging what is expedient with reference to a particular end, of which prudence is a true conception.

**THIS IS THE END OF THE
NINTH CHAPTER**

CHAPTER X

AGAIN the faculty of intelligence and its contrary, in virtue of which we call men intelligent or unintelligent, are not the same as science generally nor as opinion. For then all men would be intelligent. Nor is it identical with any one specific science, such as medicine, which deals with matters of health, or geometry, which deals with magnitudes, for intelligence is not concerned with such things as are eternal and immutable, nor with events of every kind; but only with those that a man may doubt and deliberate about.

And so it has to do with the same matters as prudence; yet the two faculties are not identical. Prudence has the capacity for commanding and taking the initiative, for its end is what should or should not be done; while intelligence is purely critical; for there is no difference between intelligence and good intelligence, or between intelligent people and people of good intelligence. Intelligence is neither the possession nor the acquisition of prudence; but just as a learner is said to be intelligent when he makes use of his scientific knowledge, so in the domain of prudence a man is said to show intelligence when he makes use of the opinions which he learns from others to form a judgment and a proper judgment; for a proper judgment is the same thing as a good judgment. It is from this use of the term in regard to learning that the word intelligence, in virtue of which men are said to be intelligent, is derived, for we often speak of learning as intelligence. Judgment or consideration, as it is called, in respect of which we say that men are considerate and show consideration, consists in a correct discernment of that which is equitable. This is shown by the fact that we regard the equitable man as disposed to show forbearance, and to show such forbearance in certain cases is considered equitable. But forbearance is judgment which correctly and truly discerns that which is equitable.

THIS IS THE END OF THE TENTH CHAPTER

NOW all these faculties which we have enumerated not unnaturally tend in the same direction. We apply the terms, judgment, intelligence, prudence, reason, to the same people, and say that they have acquired judgment and reason, and that they are prudent and intelligent. For all these faculties deal with ultimate and particular facts; and it is in virtue of his aptitude for deciding on matters which come within the province of prudence that we call a man intelligent, or a man of sound or considerate judgment.

For to act equitably in transactions with their fellows is the common characteristic of all good men.

And all matters of action are always ultimate and particular facts, for it is the business of the prudent man to know them, and intelligence and judgment are concerned with matters of action, that is, with ultimate facts.

The intuitive reason, moreover, deals with ultimate truths in both senses of the word, for the first and last terms are apprehended by the intuitive reason, and not by demonstration, and while, on the one hand, in demonstrative reasonings it apprehends the immutable first terms; on the other hand, in practical matters, it apprehends the ultimate or contingent fact which forms the minor premiss.

It is from reflection upon such facts, that we arrive at our conception of the final cause or end of life, the universal principle being derived from the particular facts. These particular facts, therefore, must be apprehended by perception, that is, in other words, by intuitive reason.

And for this reason these faculties are thought to be natural; and that while no man is thought to be naturally wise, men are thought to be naturally endowed with judgment, intelligence and reason. This is proved by the fact that these faculties are regarded as accompanying certain periods of life, and that a certain age is said to give reason and judgment, as if nature were the cause. And thus the intuitive reason is both the beginning and end, for demonstration both starts from, and is concerned with, these ultimate truths.

And so we should attend to the undemonstrated assertions and opinions of men of age and experience and prudence, no less than to their demonstrations, for they see aright, having gained their power of moral vision from experience.

THIS IS THE END OF THE
ELEVENTH CHAPTER

CHAPTER XII

E have now stated the nature and objects of prudence and wisdom respectively, and that each is a virtue of a different part of the soul. But, it may be asked, what is their utility? For wisdom does not concern itself with any of the causes of human happiness, as it has nothing to do with producing any thing. Prudence indeed does regard happiness, but where is the need of it, since its province is those things which are just and honourable, and good for man, and these are the things which the good man naturally does. But we are not a bit the more apt to do them, because we know them, if the moral virtues are habits, just as we are not more apt to be healthy or in good condition from mere knowledge of what relates to these, meaning, of course, things so called not from their producing the habit, but from their evidencing

36

it in a particular subject; for we are not more apt to be healthy and in good condition merely from knowing the art of medicine or training.

If it be urged, that knowing what is good does not by itself make a man prudent, but becoming good; still prudence will be no use either to those that are good, and so have it already, or to those who have it not; because it will make no difference to them, whether they have it themselves, or put themselves under the guidance of others who have, and if so we might be contented to be in respect of this as in respect of health; for though we wish to be healthy, still we do not set about learning the art of medicine.

Furthermore, it would seem to be strange, that prudence, though inferior to wisdom, must yet have a higher authority, for it is the productive faculty which rules and directs in each matter.

These then are the points which we must discuss, for hitherto we have only raised difficulties in regard to them.

Now first we may say, that both prudence and wisdom must be desirable in themselves,

since each is a virtue of one of the parts
of the soul, even if neither of them produce
results.

In the next place, we may say that they do
produce results; thus wisdom produces happiness, not in the sense in which the medical art
produces health, but in the sense in which
health itself produces health; that is to say,
wisdom being a part of virtue in its most extensive sense, its possession and exercise make
a man happy.

Next, a man performs his proper function
when he acts in accordance with prudence and
moral virtue, for while the latter gives the right
aim and direction, the former gives the right
means to its attainment. The fourth part of
the soul, the mere nutritive principle, possesses
no such virtue, for it is neither in its power to
act, nor to refrain from action.

But to answer the objection that prudence
makes us no more apt to do what is noble and
just, we must begin a little deeper, making
this our starting-point. Just as we say, that
men may do things in themselves just, and
yet not be just men; as, for instance, when

men do what the laws require of them, either against their will, or by reason of ignorance or something else, at all events not for the sake of the things themselves; and yet they do what they ought, and all that the good man should do; so it seems, that to be a good man one must do each act in a particular frame of mind, that is, from moral purpose and for the sake of the actions themselves. Now it is virtue which secures the correctness of the moral purpose, but the means that are naturally required to carry out that purpose do not come under the province of virtue, but a different faculty. We must halt, as it were, awhile, and speak more clearly on these points.

There is then a certain faculty which is called cleverness: it is the faculty of hitting upon the means to any proposed end, and so attaining it. If then the end be a good one, the faculty is praiseworthy; if bad, it is unscrupulousness. Accordingly we apply the term clever both to the prudent and the unscrupulous.

Now prudence is not identical with cleverness, nor yet is it without this faculty. But this eye of the soul, as we may call it, does

not attain its perfect state without virtue, as
we said before, and as is quite plain, for all
syllogisms which relate to action have this
major premiss, 'since the end or the chief
good is so and so,' whatever it may be; any
definition of the good will do for the sake of
argument.   But the supreme good is seen only
by the good man; for vice distorts the moral
vision, and causes men to be deceived in regard
to the principles of action.

It is clear, therefore, that a man cannot be
prudent without being good.

We must then again resume our consideration of virtue; for it may be divided into
natural virtue and perfect virtue, which two
bear to each other a relation similar to that
which prudence bears to cleverness, one not
of identity but resemblance.   We speak of
natural virtue, for it seems that each of the
moral qualities are in some way innate in us
all.   We are just, temperate, and brave, for
instance, from our very birth; but still we seek
goodness in its highest sense as something distinct from this, and expect to find these qualities
in another form.   For even children and brutes

possess these natural virtues, which, however, are plainly hurtful without the guidance of reason. So much, at least, is matter of actual experience and observation, that as a strong body devoid of sight must, if set in motion, fall violently, because it has not sight, so it is also with natural virtue: but if it can acquire reason, it then excels in action. Just so, the natural virtue being like this strong body, will then be perfect virtue, when it too is under the guidance of reason.

So that, as in the case of the reasoning part of the soul, there are two forms, cleverness and prudence; so also, in the case of the moral part, there are two, natural virtue and perfect virtue ; and of these the latter is impossible without prudence.

This leads some people to say, that all the virtues are forms of prudence, and Socrates was partly right in his inquiry, and partly wrong ; he was wrong, in thinking that all the virtues are forms of prudence, and right in saying that they are impossible without prudence.

This is proved by the fact that nowadays everybody in defining virtue, after stating the

subjects to which it is related, adds that it is the
moral state which accords with right reason :
' right' meaning in accordance with prudence.
So then it seems that everybody has an instinc-
tive notion, that that state which is in accordance with prudence is virtue ; however we must
make a slight change in this expression, for
virtue is not merely that state which is in
accordance with right reason, but that state
which implies the possession of right reason ;
which, in such matters, is prudence.   The
difference between us and Socrates is this ; he
thought the virtues were reasoning processes,
that is, that they were all sciences, but we say
that they imply the possession of reason.

From what has been said, then, it is clear
that one cannot be, strictly speaking, good without prudence, or prudent without moral virtue.

And by the distinction between natural and
perfect virtue, we can meet an objection which
may be urged, namely that the virtues are
found apart from one another, for the same
man is not by nature equally inclined to all
the virtues, so that he will have acquired
one virtue before he has acquired another.

We would reply, this is possible in the case of the natural virtues, but not in the case of such virtues as entitle a man to be called absolutely good ; for if the one virtue of prudence exist, all the various moral virtues will necessarily co-exist with it.

It is plain, too, that even if prudence were not practical, we should yet need it, as it is the virtue of a part of the soul ; and that the moral purpose cannot be right, without prudence or moral virtue : the latter giving us the right end, the former the correct means which conduce to the end.

Then again, prudence is not mistress of wisdom, that is, of the superior part of the soul, any more than medicine is the mistress of health ; for prudence does not make use of wisdom, but aims at producing it ; nor does it rule wisdom, but rules in its interests.

The objection is, in fact, about as valid as if a man should say that statesmanship rules the gods, because it gives orders about all things in the community.

**THIS IS THE END OF THE
TWELFTH CHAPTER**

BOOK VII

CHAPTER I

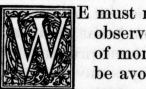E must now make a fresh start, and observe that there are three forms of moral character which ought to be avoided, namely, vice, incontinence, and brutality. In the case of the two former it is plain what the opposites are, for we call the one virtue and the other continence. As the opposite of brutality it will be most appropriate to name the virtue which is beyond us, that is, heroic or divine virtue, as Homer makes Priam say of Hector that he was exceedingly good, 'nor was he like the offspring of mortal man, but of a god.' If, then, as is commonly said, men are raised to the position of gods by reason of very high excellence in virtue, it is evident that the state which is opposite to the brutal will be of this nature; for as brutes are not virtuous or

vicious, so neither are gods, but the state of these is something more precious than virtue, of the former something different in kind from vice.

And as, on the one hand, it is a rare thing for a man to be godlike, to employ a term in use among the Lacedæmonians when they admire a man exceedingly, so the brutal man is rare among men; the character is found chiefly among barbarians, and some cases of it are the result of disease or mutilation; and to men whose vice is worse than human we apply this opprobrious term. However, we must in a subsequent place make some mention of this disposition, and vice has been already discussed. We must, therefore, now speak of incontinence and effeminacy and luxury on the one hand, and of continence and endurance on the other, for we must not regard these states as respectively identical with virtue and vice, or again as generally different from them.

And we should adopt the same course as before, that is, state the current opinions, and, after raising and discussing difficulties which suggest themselves, then establish, if possible, the truth of all the current opinions respecting these affections of the moral character; or, if not of all, of most and the most important; for if the difficulties can be solved, and the popular opinions thus confirmed, we may consider we have explained the matter sufficiently.

It is commonly thought that continence and endurance are good and praiseworthy, while incontinence and effeminacy are bad and blamable, and that the continent man is identical with one who abides by his calculations, and the incontinent man with one who departs from them; and that the incontinent man does things at the instigation of his passions, knowing them to be wrong, while the continent man, knowing his desires to be wrong, refuses, by the influence of reason, to follow their suggestions.

It is also commonly thought that the temperate man unites the qualities of continence and endurance, but while some say that every one who unites these qualities is a temperate man, others do not. And so, too, while some speak of the incontinent man as intemperate, and of the intemperate man as incontinent, others make a distinction between them.

It is sometimes said that the prudent man cannot be incontinent, at other times that some men who are prudent and clever are incontinent.

And, lastly, men are said to be incontinent even in respect of anger, and honour, and gain.

These, then, are the common statements made upon the subject.

THIS IS THE END OF THE FIRST CHAPTER

CHAPTER II

BUT it may be asked, how can a man, while judging rightly, yet act incontinently?

Some people maintain that it is impossible if he really knows what is right; for it is a strange thing, as Socrates thought, that when a man has real knowledge, something else should master him, and drag him about like a slave. Socrates, in fact, contended generally against the theory, maintaining that there is no such state as incontinence, for no one acts contrary to what is best when he knows it, and that if he does so act, it is only through ignorance of what is best.

With all due respect to Socrates, his account of the matter is at variance with plain facts, and we must enquire with regard to the affection in question, if it be caused by ignorance, what is the nature of the ignorance.

For it is plain that the man who acts incontinently, does not suppose his acts to be right before the passion seizes him.

There are people who partly agree with and partly differ from Socrates. They admit that nothing can prevail over knowledge, but they do not admit that men never act contrary to what seems best; and so they say that the incontinent man, when he is overcome by his pleasure, has merely an opinion but not knowledge.

But then, if it is opinion, and not knowledge, and if the opposing conception is not strong, but weak, as is the case when a man is in doubt, we pardon a man for not abiding by it in the face of strong desires; but we do not pardon vice, nor anything which deserves blame.

Is it, then, when prudence opposes desire, that a person is blamed for yielding. For prudence has the strongest influence. But that is absurd, for then the same man will be at once prudent and incontinent, and surely no single person would maintain that it is consistent with the character of the prudent man to voluntarily do the most disgraceful acts. Besides we have already shown, that the very mark of a man of this character is aptitude to act, as distinguished from mere knowledge of what is right; because he is a man conversant with particular details, and possessed of all the other virtues.

Again, if the existence of strong and bad desires is essential to continence, the temperate will not be continent, nor the continent man temperate; for it is inconsistent with the temperate character to have strong or bad desires. Yet the continent must have such desires. For if his desires were good, then the moral state which hinders him from following their suggestions would be bad, and so continence would not be in all cases good. If, on the other hand, they were weak and not wrong, there would be nothing noble in conquering them, nor if they were wrong and weak, would there be anything great in doing so.

Again, if continence makes a man apt to abide by every opinion without exception, it is bad, as, for instance, if it makes him abide by a false opinion : and if incontinence makes a man

apt to abandon every opinion without exception, there will be a kind of incontinence that
is good, an instance of which is Neoptolemus
in the Philoctetes of Sophocles; for he is to
be praised for not adhering to the plan which
Ulysses had persuaded him to adopt, because
of the pain which he felt at telling a lie.

Again, false sophistical reasoning presents
a difficulty : for the sophists, wishing to prove
a paradox so that they may be thought clever
if they succeed, construct a syllogism which
perplexes the hearer. For his intellect is
fettered, as he is unwilling to acquiesce in
the conclusion, because it does not please his
judgment, but is unable to continue the discussion, because he cannot disentangle the web of
sophistical reasoning.

Thus, it may be argued, that folly combined with incontinence is virtue : for by
reason of his incontinence, a man does the
opposite of that which he conceives to be good ;
but he conceives that what is really good is
bad, and ought not to be done ; and so he will
eventually do what is good, and not what is bad.

Again, the man who, from conviction, pursues and chooses things because they are pleasant, must be thought a better man than he who does so, not from conviction, but from incontinence : for he is more easily cured by reason of the possibility of his receiving a contrary conviction. But to the incontinent man we may apply the proverb, 'when water chokes you, how are you to wash it down?' For if he were convinced that what he does is right, a change in his convictions might stop his doing it; but now, though he is convinced that something else is right, nevertheless he does this.

Again, if incontinence and continence may be exhibited in every thing, who is the man who is simply called incontinent? For no one unites all the forms of incontinence, and yet there are some men of whom we speak as incontinent, without any qualification.

Such then are the difficulties which arise, and of these we must remove some, and leave others; for the solving of a difficulty is the discovery of a truth.

THIS IS THE END OF THE
SECOND CHAPTER

CHAPTER III

E must then enquire, first, whether the incontinent act with knowledge or not, and what knowledge here means; and next, what is to be regarded as the sphere of continence and incontinence, that is, whether they are concerned with pleasures and pains of all kinds, or certain definite ones; and with regard to continence and endurance, whether these are designations of the same character, or different. And in like manner we must go into all questions which are connected with the present enquiry.

But the real starting-point of the enquiry is, whether the continent and the incontinent man are distinguished by their object-matter, or by their respective relations to it. I mean, whether the incontinent man is so called merely because he is incontinent in certain things, or because he is incontinent in a certain

53

manner, or on both grounds. Next, whether
continence and incontinence may be displayed
in all things. For he who is designated incontinent without any qualification does not display his character in all things, but only in those
things with which the intemperate is concerned:
nor is he so designated merely because he is
concerned with these things, for then his
character would be identical with intemperance, but because he is concerned with these
things in a particular manner. For the intemperate man is led away of his own deliberate
moral purpose, holding that it is his line to
pursue the pleasure of the moment: while the
incontinent man does not think so, but still
pursues it all the same.

Now as to the argument that it is true
opinion and not knowledge, against which men
act incontinently, it makes no difference to the
point in question, because some of those who
only have opinions have no doubt about them,
but think they have accurate knowledge. If
then it is urged, that those who have opinions,
will be more likely to act in opposition to their
conceptions than those who have knowledge,

owing to the weakness of their belief; we would reply that there is no such difference between knowledge and opinion; for some men believe their own opinions no less firmly than others do their positive knowledge: Heraclitus is an instance of this.

But we use the word knowledge in two different senses. We say that a man knows, when he possesses knowledge, but does not use it; and also when he uses it. There will be a difference then between doing wrong, when one possesses knowledge, but does not call it into operation, and so doing when one possesses knowledge and exercises it. The latter is a strange case, but the mere having knowledge, and not exercising it, presents no anomaly.

Again, as there are two kinds of propositions affecting action, universal and particular, there is no reason why a man may not act against his knowledge, having both propositions in his mind, if he uses the universal only, and not the particular, for the particulars are the objects of moral action.

There is a difference also in universal propositions; a universal proposition may relate

partly to the person, and partly to the thing:
take the following for instance; 'dry food
is good for every man,' this may have the
two minor premisses, 'this is a man,' and
'so and so is dry food;' but whether a given
substance is so and so, a man either does
not possess the knowledge, or does not use
it. According to these different senses, there
will be an immense difference, so that for a
man to know in the one sense, and yet act
wrongly, would be nothing strange, but in
any of the other senses it would be a matter
for wonder.

Again, men may have knowledge in yet
another way than those which have just been
mentioned: for we constantly see a man's
state so differing by possessing and not using
knowledge, that he may have it in one sense,
and in another sense not have it; when a
man is asleep, for instance, or mad, or drunk.
But men who are under the influence of
passion, are in a similar condition; for anger
and sexual desire, and other such things,
evidently produce a change in the condition
of the body, and in some cases they even

cause madness. It is plain therefore that we must say that the incontinent are in a similar state to these.

And their repeating what implies knowledge is no proof of knowledge in the full sense, for those who are under the influence of these passions repeat demonstrations, and verses of Empedocles, just as children, when first learning, string words together, before they know their meaning, for the right use of language is a thing into which, as it were, one grows, and this necessarily requires time. So that we must suppose that the incontinent repeat these moral sayings, in the same way as actors say their parts.

Again, we may consider incontinence in the following way, by an examination of the actual working of the mind, as follows: all action may be analysed into a syllogism, in which the one premiss is an universal opinion, and the other, an opinion which concerns particulars, of which sense, moral or physical, as the case may be, is cognisant. Now when a third opinion results from these two, it follows necessarily that, as far as theory goes,

the mind should assent to the conclusion,
and in practical matters should immediately
act upon it.

For instance, if it is right that 'all sweet
things are to be tasted,' and this particular
thing is sweet, it follows necessarily, that he
who is able and is not hindered should not
only draw, but put in practice, the conclusion;
that is, should taste it. When then there is
in the mind one universal opinion forbidding
to taste, and another which says that all that
is sweet is pleasant, with its particular, 'this
is sweet,' and the latter is effectively present
and supported by desire, while the first universal opinion bids avoidance of the thing,
desire urges to take it; for desire has the
power of moving the various organs of the
body. And thus it appears that a person may
be said, in a certain sense, to act incontinently
under the influence of reason and opinion, an
opinion, however, that is not in itself contrary
to reason, but only accidentally so; for it is
the desire, not the opinion, that is contrary to
right reason. And this is the reason why
brutes cannot be incontinent, because they

have no universal judgments, but only images and memories of particulars.

As to the manner by which the incontinent man gets out of this ignorance and recovers his knowledge, the account will be the same as in the case of the man who is drunk or asleep, and will not be peculiar to the condition of incontinence, so for such an account we must apply to the physiologists. But as the minor premiss of every practical syllogism is an opinion about a matter of perception, and determines the actions; it follows that the incontinent man, when under the influence of passion, either does not possess it, or possesses it in a sense in which, as we explained, possession does not mean knowledge, but merely repeating words, as a drunken man might repeat the verses of Empedocles. And as the minor term is not universal, and is thought to be less a matter of knowledge than the universal term; it seems that what Socrates sought to establish is correct; that is to say, the condition of incontinence does not take place in the presence of that which is thought to be specially and properly knowledge, nor is it this kind of knowledge which incontinence perverts, but only that knowledge which is formed by perception.

So much then for the question whether a person acts incontinently with knowledge, or without, and in what sense it is possible to act incontinently with knowledge.

THIS IS THE END OF THE THIRD CHAPTER

CHAPTER IV

THE next question to be discussed is, whether a man can be incontinent simply, or whether all who are incontinent are to be accounted such, in respect of some particular thing; and, if the former be the case, what is the sphere in which his incontinence is manifested.

It is evident that pleasures and pains are the sphere in which both the continent and steadfast, and the incontinent and effeminate, display their characters.

But some things which produce pleasure are necessary, and others are desirable in themselves, but admit of excess. All bodily things which produce pleasure are necessary; such as those which relate to food and other grosser appetites, in short, those bodily things with which we said that temperance and intemperance were concerned.

61

Other things, although not necessary, are desirable in themselves; for instance, victory, honour, wealth, and such like good or pleasant things. Now those who go to excess in their liking for such things in spite of their own better reason, are not called incontinent simply, but they are called incontinent in respect of money, or gain, or honour, or anger; and not simply, because they are different, and are called incontinent only in virtue of a kind of resemblance, as when we add to a man's name, 'conqueror in the Olympic games,' the account of him as man differs but little from the account of him as the man who conquered in the Olympic games, but still it is different. And this may be proved thus; incontinence is blamed, not as an error merely, but also as being a vice, either wholly, or partially; but those who are incontinent in respect of money, gain, and the like, are not so blamed.

But of those who are concerned with those bodily enjoyments, which we say are also the object-matter of the temperate and the intemperate, he who pursues excessive pleasures, and too much avoids things which are painful, as hunger and thirst, heat and cold, and everything connected with touch and taste, and who does so not of deliberate purpose, but contrary to his moral choice and intellectual conviction, is called incontinent, not with the addition that he is incontinent with regard to any particular thing, as anger, but simply incontinent.

And a proof that the term is thus applied is, that the kindred term ' effeminate ' is used in respect of these enjoyments, but not in respect of wealth, gain, honour, and the like. And for this reason we rank the incontinent and intemperate, the continent and temperate, under the same head; but not any of the others, because the former are in a manner concerned with the same pleasures and pains. But though they are concerned with the same things, their attitude is different; the intemperate act with deliberate purpose, but the incontinent do not. And so we should say, that man is more entirely given up to his passions, who, without desire or without any strong desire, pursues excessive pleasures, and avoids moderate pains, than the man who does so, because his desire is very strong. For what would the former be likely to do, if he had the additional stimulus of youthful desire, and if it were violent pain to him to forego those pleasures, which we have denominated necessary.

But some desires and pleasures are noble; for, as we said before, some pleasant things are naturally desirable, such as money, gain, honour, victory, others the opposite of these, and others intermediate. In regard both to these and to the intermediate, men are blamed not merely for being affected by them, or desiring or liking them, but only for exceeding in any way in these feelings.

So those people are blamed, who, in spite of reason, are mastered by, or pursue, to an unreasonable extent, some noble and good object; they, for instance, who are too much devoted to honour, or to their children or parents; not but what these are good objects, and men are praised for their devotion to them; but still they admit of excess, for instance, if one should fight even against the gods like Niobe, or like Satyrus who was nicknamed 'the filial' from his affection for his father, which he carried to a foolish pitch.

It is true that these matters do not admit of vice, for the reason assigned, that all these are objects that are desirable in themselves, though excess in them is wrong, and is to be avoided : similarly, these matters do not admit of incontinence; for incontinence is not merely a thing that ought to be avoided, but is actually blamable.

But because of the resemblance of the affection to incontinence, we use the term incontinence in these cases, but with a qualification, as when we call a man a bad physician, or bad actor, although we should not think of calling him bad in an absolute sense. As then in these cases we do not apply the term simply, or without qualification, because neither of the states in question is a vice, but only analogous to a vice, so it is plain, that we must understand that only to be continence or incontinence in a strict sense which has the same sphere as temperance and intemperance, and that these terms are applied

II. E

in the case of anger only by analogy: for which reason, we call a man 'incontinent in anger,' as 'in honour' or 'in gain,' adding a qualification.

THIS IS THE END OF THE
FOURTH CHAPTER

CHAPTER V

AS there are some things naturally pleasant, and of these, two kinds; those, namely, which are pleasant generally, and those which are so relatively to particular kinds of animals and men; so there are others which are not naturally pleasant, but which come to be so in consequence either of physical defects, or custom, or depraved natural tastes; and in each of these kinds of pleasure, we may observe corresponding moral states.

I mean brutal states, as in the case of the female, who, they say, would rip up women with child and devour the children; or the tastes which are found among the savage tribes bordering on the Pontus, some liking raw flesh, and some being cannibals, and some giving one another their children to make feasts of; or what is said of Phalaris. There are brutal states caused in some by

disease or madness; like the man who sacri-
ficed and ate his mother, or the slave who
devoured the liver of his fellow-servant.
Others again are caused by disease or by
custom, as, for instance, plucking out one's
hair, or biting one's nails, or eating coals
and earth. Wherever nature is really the
cause of these habits, no one would think
of calling people who give way to them incontinent, and the same is the case with
those in whom habit has produced a morbid
state.

Habits of this kind, then, like brutality
itself, lie beyond the pale of vice; but when
a man who has these morbid desires, con-
quers or is conquered by them, this is not to
be called continence or incontinence in an
absolute sense, but only metaphorically, just
as the man who is mastered by his angry
passions, cannot be called incontinent in an
absolute sense. For all excessive folly,
cowardice, intemperance and rage, are either
brutal or morbid. The man, for instance,
who is naturally afraid of all things, even if
a mouse should stir, is cowardly after a

brutish sort; there was a man again who, by reason of disease, was afraid of a cat. Again, foolish people, who are naturally destitute of reason, and live only by their senses, are to be called brutal, as are some tribes of remote barbarians, but foolish people who are so from disease, for instance, epilepsy, or insanity, are morbidly irrational.

A man may sometimes merely have one of these impulses without being mastered by it, as for instance if Phalaris had restrained his unnatural desire to eat a child: or he may both have the impulse and be mastered by it. As then human vice is called vice in an absolute sense, while the other is so called with the addition of 'brutal' or 'morbid,' so it is clear that incontinence may be either brutal or morbid, but it is only incontinence simply when it is co-extensive with human intemperance.

THIS IS THE END OF THE
FIFTH CHAPTER

CHAPTER VI

I T is plain then, that incontinence and continence have to do only with those things with which intemperance and temperance have to do, and that in other matters there is another kind of incontinence which is so called metaphorically, and not absolutely. We will now proceed to show that incontinence in anger is less disgraceful than incontinence in desires.

In the first place, it seems that anger does, in a way, listen to reason, but mishears it; like hasty servants who run out before they have heard the whole of what is said, and so mistake the order; or like dogs, who bark at the slightest noise, before they have seen whether it be friend or foe; just so, our angry passions, from their natural heat and quickness, hearing something, but not hearing the command of reason, rush to take revenge.

For when reason or imagination shows that
an insult or slight has been given, the angry
passion infers that it ought to fight against
the offender and fires up immediately; whereas desire, if reason or sense, as the case may
be, merely says a thing is pleasant, rushes to
the enjoyment of it. And so anger obeys reason
in a manner, but desire does not. Desire
therefore is more disgraceful: for he who
is incontinent in anger, yields in a manner
to reason, but the other yields to his desire,
and not to reason at all.

Again, it is more excusable to follow
natural impulses, just as it is more excusable
to follow such desires as are common to all
men, and the more common they are, the
more excusable are they also. But anger
and rage are more natural than the desires
of excessive and unnecessary pleasures, as
we see in the story of the man who defended
himself for beating his father. 'My father,'
he said, 'used to beat his, and his father his
again, and this little fellow here,' pointing to
his child, 'will beat me when he is grown a
man: it runs in the family.' And, then, there

is the story of the man who was being dragged
out of the house by his son, and bade him
stop at the door, because he himself had been
used to drag his father so far, but no further.

Again, the more the cunning employed,
the greater always is the injustice. Now the
passionate man is not cunning, nor is anger,
but quite open. Desire is cunning; as they
say of Venus, 'Cyprus-born goddess, weaver
of deceits,' and Homer says of her em-
broidered girdle, 'Persuasiveness cheating
the subtlest mind.' And so if this kind of
incontinence is more unjust, then it is also
more disgraceful than incontinence in anger,
and is to be called incontinence in an absolute
sense, and a form of vice.

Again, no man feels pain when he commits a wanton outrage, but every one who
acts in anger feels pain in the act; whereas
he who commits a wanton outrage, does it
with pleasure. If then those things are
most unjust with which it is most just to
be angry, then incontinence in desire is more
unjust than incontinence in anger: for wanton
outrage is never done in anger.

It is clear then that incontinence in respect of the desires is more disgraceful than incontinence in respect of anger, and that continence and incontinence proper are concerned with bodily desires and pleasures. But we must take into account the differences in these desires and pleasures: for, as was said at the commencement, some are proper to the human race, and natural both in kind and degree, others are brutal, and others are caused by physical defects and diseases.

Now it is with the first of these only that temperance and intemperance are concerned; and therefore we never speak of brutes as being either temperate or intemperate, except metaphorically, and whenever any one kind of animal is absolutely distinguished from another by peculiar wantonness, insolence, mischievousness, or voracity, for they do not possess moral purpose or reasoning power, but are in an unnatural state, like madmen.

Brutality is a lesser evil than vice, but it is more formidable, for it is not the corruption of the highest principle in brutes, as it

is in the human creature, but its non-exist-
ence.

It is much the same, therefore, as to compare an inanimate with an animate being, to
see which is the worse: for the badness of
that which has no principle of origination is
always less harmful; and reason is such a
principle. A similar case would be the com-
paring injustice with an unjust man; for in a
certain sense each of them is worse than the
other. For a bad man would do ten thousand
times as much harm as a brute.

THIS IS THE END OF THE
SIXTH CHAPTER

CHAPTER VII

UT with regard to the pleasures and pains of touch and taste, and the corresponding desires and aversions with which, as we determined before, intemperance and temperance are concerned, one may be so disposed as to yield to temptations, to which most men would be superior, or to be superior to those to which most men would yield: in respect of pleasures, the former of these characters is called incontinent, and the latter continent; and in respect of pains, the former is said to show effeminacy, and the latter, endurance. The moral state of most men is something between the two, even if they incline rather to the worse.

But, since some pleasures are necessary and some are not, or are so only to a certain degree, but not the excess or defect of them, and similarly also with desires and pains, the

man who pursues pleasures to excess, or such
pleasures as are in themselves excess, or pursues them from moral purpose, for their own
sake, and not for the sake of any thing that
results from them, is intemperate; for such
a man must be incapable of repentance, and,
therefore incurable, because he that is incapable of repentance is incurable. He that
has too little love of pleasure is deficient,
while he who observes the mean is temperate.
So with the man who avoids bodily pains, not
because he cannot endure them, but because
he chooses not to withstand them.

But of those who act thus without moral
purpose, the one is led on by reason of
pleasure, the other because he avoids the
pain it would cost him to withstand his
desire; and so they are different the one
from the other. Now every one would pro-
nounce a man worse for doing something disgraceful without any, or with a very slight,
impulse of desire, than for doing the same
from the impulse of a very strong desire,
for striking a man when not angry, than if
he did so in anger: because one naturally

says, 'What would he have done had he been under the influence of passion?' And on this ground, the intemperate man is worse than the incontinent man. Of the two characters which have been mentioned, the one is rather a kind of effeminacy, the other is incontinent.

The character of incontinence is opposed to that of continence, and that of endurance to that of effeminacy; for enduring consists in continued resistance, and continence in actual mastery. And continued resistance and actual mastery are different in the same manner as not being conquered differs from gaining a victory; and so continence is preferable to endurance.

But he who gives way to those temptations, which the generality of men can and do resist, is effeminate and luxurious, for luxury is a form of effeminacy. Such a man will let his robe drag in the dirt to avoid the trouble of lifting it up, or will play the invalid without considering himself wretched, though he is like one who is wretched. So it is too with continence and incontinence. If a man yields to pleasures or pains which are violent and excessive, it is no matter for wonder, but rather for pardon, if he made what resistance he could; like Philoctetes in Theodectes' drama, when bitten by the viper; or like Cercyon in the Alope of Carcinus, or like men who in trying to suppress their laughter burst into a loud continuous fit of it, as happened to Xenophantus. But it is a matter for wonder when a man yields to, and cannot contend against, those pleasures or pains which the generality of men are able to resist, unless his failure be due to natural constitution or disease, as is the case with the Scythian kings, whose effeminacy is hereditary, or with women, who are naturally weaker than men.

The man who is a slave to amusement is commonly thought to be intemperate, but he really is effeminate; for amusement is a kind of relaxation, as it is a rest from labour, and the character in question is one of those who exceed due bounds in respect of this.

There are two forms of incontinence, the hasty, and the weak. Some men deliberate, but under the influence of passion do not abide by the result of their deliberation; others again, do not deliberate, and are therefore led away by passion. While there are some who, like those who by tickling themselves beforehand get rid of ticklishness, having felt and seen beforehand the approach of temptation, and roused up themselves and their resolution, yield not to passion; whether it be pleasant or painful. Those who are constitutionally of a quick or melancholy temperament, are most liable to incontinence of the hasty sort, for the former from the rapidity, and the latter from the violence of their passions, do not wait for reason, because they are disposed to follow their imaginations.

The intemperate man, as was observed before, is not given to repentance: for he abides by his moral purpose: but the incontinent man is always open to repentance. And so the case is not as we determined it before, but the former is incurable, and the latter may be cured; for depravity is like chronic diseases, dropsy and consumption, for instance, but incontinence is like epilepsy: the former being a chronic evil, the latter intermittent. In fact, incontinence and vice are generically different, for vice acts imperceptibly but incontinence does not act imperceptibly.

But of the different forms of incontinence, those who are carried off their feet by a sudden access of temptation, are better than those who possess reason, but do not abide by it, as they are not overcome by so strong a passion, nor do they act wholly without premeditation, like the others. For the incontinent man is like those who are soon intoxicated and with a little wine, that is, with less than most men.

It is plain, then, that incontinence is not vice; and yet perhaps there is a sense in which it is a vice, for the former is contrary to moral purpose, and the latter is according to it, but still they come to much the same thing as regards actions. The case is much like what Demodocus said of the Milesians, 'the Milesians are not fools, but they do just the kind of things that fools do;' and so the incontinent are not unjust, but they do unjust acts.

The incontinent man then is the kind of character to pursue bodily pleasures which are in excess, and contrary to right reason, without being convinced of their goodness, but the intemperate man is convinced that they are good, because it is his character to pursue these pleasures; the former may be easily persuaded to a different course, but the latter not, for virtue and vice respectively preserve and destroy the moral principle; but the motive is the principle or starting-point in moral actions, just as axioms and postulates are in mathematics: and neither in morals, nor mathematics, is it reason which is apt to teach the principles; but virtue, either natural or acquired, which teaches to hold right opinions about the principle. He in whom this virtue then is to be found is the temperate man, and he in whom it is not found is intemperate.

But there is a class of people who are apt to be so carried away by passion as to act contrary to right reason, they are so far overcome by passion, that they do not act in accordance with right reason, but not so far

II. F

overcome as to be convinced that they ought to pursue such pleasures without limit. These are the incontinent, who are better than the intemperate, and not absolutely bad: for in them the highest and best part in our nature, that is, principle, is preserved. To these are opposed another class of people, who are apt to abide by their resolutions, and not to depart from them; at all events, not at the instigation of passion.

It is evident then from these considerations, that the latter is a good state, and the former bad.

THIS IS THE END OF THE
SEVENTH CHAPTER

NEXT comes the question, is a man continent if he abides by his reason and moral purpose, whatever they may be, or only if he abides by a right purpose? and again, is a man incontinent if he does not abide by his reason and moral purpose, whatever they may be? or, to put the case as we did before, is it only if he does not abide by true reason and right moral purpose?

Is not this the truth, that though incidentally it may be by reason and moral purpose of any kind, that the one character abides, and the other does not, yet essentially it is true reason and right moral purpose by which the one does, and the other does not abide? For if a man chooses or pursues A for the sake of B, he is said to pursue and choose B essentially, but A only incidentally. For by 'essentially' we mean 'absolutely' or 'simply,' and so, in a way, it is opinion of any kind soever which the one abides by and the other abandons, but absolutely or simply it is true opinion.

There are also people, who abide fixedly by their own opinions, and they are commonly called obstinate, as they are hard to persuade, and their convictions are not easily changed. These people bear some resemblance to the continent, as does the prodigal to the liberal, or the foolhardy to the courageous, but they are different in many respects. The continent man does not change by reason of passion and desire, yet when occasion so requires, he will be easily persuaded; but the obstinate man will not listen to reason, though many of this class often conceive strong desires, and are led by their pleasures. The opinionated, the ignorant, and the boorish are all obstinate: the first, from motives of pleasure and pain, for they have the pleasurable feeling of a kind of victory in refusing to be convinced, and they are pained when their decrees, so to speak, are reversed; so that, in fact, they rather resemble the incontinent man than the continent.

There are also some who abandon their resolutions, but the reason is not incontinence; as, for instance, Neoptolemus in the Philoctetes of Sophocles. It was indeed pleasure which was his motive in abandoning his resolution, but then it was one of a noble sort: for it was noble in his eyes to be truthful, and he had been persuaded by Ulysses to lie.

So it is not every one who acts from the motive of pleasure that is intemperate or wicked, or incontinent, but only he who acts from the impulse of a base pleasure.

**THIS IS THE END OF THE
EIGHTH CHAPTER**

CHAPTER IX

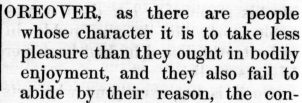OREOVER, as there are people whose character it is to take less pleasure than they ought in bodily enjoyment, and they also fail to abide by their reason, the continent then are those who come between these and the incontinent. For the incontinent fail to abide by their reason, because of some excess, and the former, because of some deficiency; while the continent man does abide by reason, and is not influenced by the excess or by the deficiency.

But if continence is a good thing, it follows that both the states opposed to it must be bad, as indeed they plainly are; but because one of these states is seen in few cases, and very rarely, continence comes to be regarded as the only opposite of incontinence, just as temperance is thought to be the only opposite of intemperance.

Again, as many names are used metaphorically, so people have come to speak metaphorically of the continence of the temperate man; for the continent man and the temperate man have this in common, that they do nothing contrary to right reason on the impulse of bodily pleasures, but whereas the former has bad desires, the latter has not; and whereas the latter is so constituted as not even to feel pleasure contrary to his reason, the former is so constituted as to feel such pleasure, but will not be led away by it.

The incontinent man and the intemperate man also resemble each other, though they are different; both pursue bodily pleasures, but the latter pursues them thinking that it is right, while the former pursues them not thinking so.

It is impossible for the same man to be at once prudent and incontinent: for it has been shown that a man cannot be prudent without being at the same time morally good. Again, a man is not prudent merely because he knows what is good, he must also be able to act up to his knowledge, but the incontinent man is not able to act up to his knowledge. But there is no reason why the clever man should not be incontinent; and the reason why some men are occasionally thought to be prudent, and yet incontinent, is this, that cleverness differs from prudence in the way described in a former book, resembling it so far as the intellectual element is concerned, but differing from it in respect of the moral purpose.

Nor is the incontinent man like one who has knowledge and uses it, but like one who, having knowledge, is overpowered by sleep or wine. He acts voluntarily, for he knows, in a certain sense, what he is doing, and with what object, but he is not a confirmed bad man, as his moral purpose is good; he may therefore be said to be only half bad. Nor is the incontinent man unjust, for he does not act with deliberate intent: inasmuch as he is either incapable of abiding by his deliberate resolutions, or else he is incapable of deliberating at all.

The incontinent man, then, resembles a

state which always makes excellent decrees, and has admirable laws, but does not act on them, according to the jest of Anaxandrides, 'That State did will it, which cares nought for laws.' The bad man, on the other hand, resembles a state which acts upon its laws, but whose laws are bad.

Incontinence and continence, after all, are concerned with something beyond the average moral state of men; for the continent man is more true to his reason, and the incontinent man less so, than is in the power of most men.

Of the various forms of incontinence, that of the melancholy temperament is more easily curable than that of those who form resolutions and break them; and that incontinence which is the result of habit is more curable than that which originates in natural infirmity; for of course it is easier to change habit than nature. For the very reason why habit is so hard to alter is that it resembles nature; as Evenus says,

'Practice, I say, my friend, doth long endure,
  And at the last is even very nature.'

We have now discussed the nature of continence and incontinence, of endurance and effeminacy, and the mutual relation of these states of mind.

THIS IS THE END OF THE
NINTH CHAPTER

BOOK VIII

CHAPTER I

NEXT it would seem proper to discuss friendship. For friendship is a kind of virtue, or at any rate implies virtue, and it is a thing most necessary to our life, for no one would choose to live without friends, though he should have all the other good things in the world. And, in fact, it is when men are rich, and possessed of authority and influence, that they seem to have special need of friends; for where is the use of such prosperity, if there be taken away the doing of kindnesses, of which friends are the most usual and most commendable objects? Or how can it be kept or preserved without friends, for the greater it is, the more precarious will it be. In poverty moreover, and all other adversities, we regard our friends as our only refuge.

We need friends when we are young, to keep us from error; when we are old, to tend us and to do for us what we are too feeble to do for ourselves; and in the prime of life, to help us in noble deeds; as Homer says, 'two together,' for we are thus more able to devise plans, and carry them out.

Again, it seems to be implanted in us by nature: as, for instance, in the parent towards the offspring, and in the offspring towards the parent, not merely in the human species, but likewise in birds and most animals, and in those of the same race towards one another, and specially among men; for which reason we commend those who love their fellow-men. And one may see in the course of travel, how close of kin and how friendly man is to man.

Friendship, moreover, seems to be the bond that holds states together, and legislators seem to be more anxious to secure it than justice. For concord is akin to friendship, and it is concord which they certainly aim at securing, and dissension which they seek to banish as an enemy.

If people are friends, justice is not

required; but, on the other hand, people may be just, and yet need friendship as well. Indeed, it seems that justice in its highest forms partakes of the nature of friendship.

But not only is friendship indispensable, it is also noble; for we praise those who love their friends, and to have numerous friends is thought to be a noble thing; some go so far as to hold, that 'good man' and 'friend' are synonymous terms.

**THIS IS THE END OF THE
FIRST CHAPTER**

CHAPTER II

ET there are not a few differences
of opinion concerning friendship.
Some men hold that it is a kind
of resemblance, and that men who
are like one another are friends :
whence come the common sayings, 'like to
like,' 'birds of a feather,' and so on. Others,
on the contrary, say that 'two of a trade
never agree.'

Again, some men carry their enquiries on
these points higher, and reason physically : as
Euripides, who says,
'The earth by drought consumed doth love
   the rain,
And the great heaven, overcharged with rain,
  Doth love to fall in showers upon the earth.'
Heraclitus, again, maintains that 'contrariety
is expedient, and that the best agreement
arises from things differing, and that all things
come into being in the way of the principle
of antagonism.'

Empedocles, among others, in direct opposition to these, affirms that 'like desires like.'

These physical questions we will dismiss, inasmuch as they are foreign to the present enquiry; and we will examine such as refer to man, and concern moral characters and emotions: as, for instance, 'whether friendship can exist among all men alike, or whether it is impossible for bad men to be friends,' and 'whether there is only one kind of friendship, or several.' For it would seem that those who hold the opinion that there is but one kind of friendship, because it admits of degrees, base their opinion upon insufficient grounds; for things which are different in kind admit likewise of degrees. But we have spoken already on this point.

**THIS IS THE END OF THE
SECOND CHAPTER**

CHAPTER III

THE difficulty as to the various kinds of friendship will perhaps be cleared up when we have ascertained what it is that is the object of friendship or love. For it seems that it is not every thing indiscriminately which is loved, but only that which is lovable, and that the lovable is either good, or pleasant, or useful. Now it would seem that a thing is useful if it helps us to gain something good or pleasant, and so the good and the pleasant will be lovable considered as ends.

The question then arises: whether it is that which is good absolutely, or that which is good for themselves, that men love. For there is sometimes a difference between them, and the same question may be asked in regard to the pleasant. It seems, then, that each individual loves that which is good for himself, and that while the good is lovable in itself, that is lovable to each individual which is good for him. It may be said that each individual loves not that which is really good for him, but that which appears good relatively to himself. But this will make no real difference, for the lovable will then be that which appears to be lovable.

There are, then, three motives of friendship or love: but the term is not applied to the case of fondness for inanimate things, because there is no requital of the affection, nor desire for the good of those objects: it certainly savours of the ridiculous to say that a man fond of wine wishes well to it: the only sense in which it is true being that he wishes it to be kept safe and sound for his own use and benefit. But in the case of a friend we say that we ought to wish him good for his own sake. And men who do thus wish the good of another are called well - disposed, when the feeling is not reciprocated; it is called friendship when the well-wishing is reciprocated. But must we not add that the well-wishing must be mutu-

II. G

ally known? for a man often wishes well to those whom he has never seen, but whom he supposes to be good or useful: and one of these may entertain the same sentiment towards him.

These two, then, are plainly well-disposed towards one another: but how can one call them friends, when their mutual feelings are unknown to one another? To complete the idea of friendship, then, it is requisite that they must be well-disposed towards one another, and must wish one another good from one of the motives mentioned, and that these kindly feelings should be mutually known.

THIS IS THE END OF THE THIRD CHAPTER

CHAPTER IV

S the motives of friendship differ in kind, so do the respective affections and friendships. The kinds of friendship, then, are three, equal in number to the motives of it, as any one of these can give rise to a 'mutual affection mutually known.'

Now those who love one another desire one another's good, according to the motive of their love; accordingly, they whose love for one another is founded on utility do not love one another for what they are in themselves, but only in so far as they receive some good one from another.

It is the same with those whose love is based on pleasure. People are fond of witty men, not because they are of a particular character, but because they are pleasant to themselves. So then they whose love is

99

founded on utility, love their friends for what is good to themselves; they whose love is based upon pleasure, do so for what is pleasant to themselves; that is to say, they love a person not for being what he is in himself, but for being useful or pleasant. These friendships, then, are accidental: for the object is not beloved for what he is, but for what he brings, advantage or pleasure, as the case may be.

Such friendships are, of course, easily dissolved, if the parties do not continue always the same; for if they are no longer pleasant or useful to one another, they cease to be friends. Now, it is the nature of utility not to be permanent, but constantly varying: so, of course, when the motive of their friendship is gone, the friendship is likewise dissolved; since it existed only for this particular object.

Friendship of this kind seems to exist principally among elderly men; for men at that time of life pursue not what is pleasurable, but what is profitable, and between young and middle-aged men who have a keen eye to their own advantage. Friends of this kind have no intimate intercourse with one another; for sometimes they are not even pleasant to one another : nor, in fact, do they desire such intercourse, unless they are profitable to one another, and they are pleasant only in so far as they have hopes of advantage. With these friendships is commonly ranked that of hospitality.

But the friendship of the young is thought to be based on pleasure; for they live at the beck and call of passion, and generally pursue what is pleasant to themselves at the moment : and as their age advances, so likewise do their pleasures change.

This is the reason why they form and dissolve friendships rapidly; for the friendship changes with the object which pleases them, and pleasure of this kind is quick to change.

The young, also, easily fall in love; love being, in great measure, a matter of impulse, and based on pleasure : and hence they form strong attachments, and quickly break them off, changing many times in the same day.

Friends of this kind, however, wish to spend their time together, and to live together, as it is thus they attain the object of their friendship.

**THIS IS THE END OF THE
FOURTH CHAPTER**

CHAPTER V

PERFECT friendship, then, is that friendship which subsists between those who are good, and have the same virtues, for such people equally wish each other's good, in so far as they are good, and they are good in themselves. And those who wish well to their friends for their friends' sake, are friends in the highest sense, for they feel thus towards them on account of what they are in themselves, and not on account of any accidental quality; so their friendship continues as long as their virtue, and virtue is a lasting thing.

Moreover, each of them is not only absolutely good, but good to his friend: for good men are not only absolutely good, but also good and useful to one another. In the same manner they are pleasant too; for all good men are both pleasant in themselves, and also to one another, inasmuch as to each individual those actions are pleasant which correspond to his nature, and all such as are like them. And the actions of good men are always the same, or at least similar.

Friendship of this kind is permanent, as we might expect, since it combines in itself all the requisite conditions of friendship. For every kind of friendship is based upon some good or some pleasure, either absolutely or relatively to the person entertaining the sentiment of friendship, and depends upon a similarity of some sort: but in this case all the requisite conditions belong to the friends in themselves, for here there is similarity, and so on, and that which is absolutely good and that which is absolutely pleasant, and these are especially the objects of affection; so it is between such people that the truest and best love and friendship is found.

It is probable that friendships of this kind will be rare, for men of this kind are rare. Besides, all requisite qualifications being presupposed, there is also required time and familiar intercourse: for, as the proverb says, men cannot know one another 'till they

have eaten the proper amount of salt together;' nor can they, in fact, admit one
another to intimacy, much less be friends,
till each has shown himself lovable to the
other, and has gained his confidence. Those
who speedily commence to treat one another
as friends, may be said to wish to be friends,
but they are not so, unless they are not only
lovable, but know one another to be so:
that is to say, a desire for friendship may
arise quickly, but not friendship itself.

This kind of friendship, then, is perfect,
both in point of time, and in all other respects;
and each friend receives from the other the
same or similar services; as ought to be the
case with friends.

The friendship which is based upon pleasure is, so to say, a copy of this, as the good
are sources of pleasure to one another;
and that based on utility is so likewise, the
good being also useful to one another. And
in these cases friendships are most likely to
be permanent when that which each receives from the other is the same—pleasure,
for instance; and not merely the same, but

arising from the same source, as in the case of two witty men; and not as it is in that of a lover and his beloved. For they do not derive their pleasure from the same thing; the pleasure of the lover is in seeing his beloved, and that of the beloved in receiving the attentions of the lover; but when the bloom of youth fades, the friendship sometimes ceases also, because then the lover derives no pleasure from seeing his beloved, and the object of his affection ceases to receive the attentions which were paid before. But, on the other hand, people frequently continue friends, if, being of similar character, they have come from custom to like one another's disposition.

People who, in matters of love, do not exchange pleasure but profit, are less truly and less permanently friends. In fact, they who are friends because of advantage commonly part when the advantage ceases: for, in reality, they never were friends of one another, but of the advantage.

So, then, it appears that, from motives of pleasure or profit, bad men may be friends to one another, or good men to bad men, or men of neutral character to one of any character whatever : but it is plain that only the good can be friends for the sake of one another, as bad men take no pleasure in one another, unless some advantage arises.

The friendship of good men, too, is the only kind that is superior to calumny; for people are not ready to believe what anyone says about one whom they have long tried and proved. Between good men there is mutual confidence, and the feeling that one's friend would never have done one wrong, and all other such things as are expected in friendship really worthy the name; but in the other kinds there is nothing to prevent all such suspicions.

For since men commonly give the name of friends to those who are connected from motives of profit (which is justified by political language, for alliances between states are thought to be contracted with a view to advantage), and also to those who are attached to one another by the motive of pleasure (as children are), we may, perhaps, also be allowed to call such persons friends, and say there are several kinds of friendship; primarily and specially the friendship of good men, in that they are good men, and the others only because of a resemblance to this. For these other people are called friends, in so far as their relation involves something that is good which constitutes a resemblance; for we must remember that the pleasant is good to those who love pleasure.

These secondary forms of friendship, however, do not altogether coincide; that is to say, the same persons do not become friends for the sake both of profit and pleasure, as these accidental properties are not often combined. And friendship having been divided into these kinds, it may be said that bad men will be friends for the sake of pleasure or profit, this being their point of resemblance; while the good are friends for one another's sake, that is, in so far as they are good.

These, then, may be termed friends, in an absolute sense, the others are friends accidentally, and so far as they resemble these.

THIS IS THE END OF THE FIFTH CHAPTER

CHAPTER VI

JUST as in the case of the different virtues, some men are termed good in respect of a certain moral state, others in respect of actions, so is it in the case of friendship. Those who live together, take pleasure in, and do good to, one another; but those who are asleep, or are locally separated, are capable of performing friendly acts, but do not actually perform them: for distance does not destroy friendship itself, but only prevents the manifestation of it in friendly acts: yet, if the absence be protracted, it is thought to cause a forgetfulness even of the friendship: and hence it has been said, 'many and many a friendship hath want of intercourse destroyed.'

Accordingly, neither the old nor the morose appear to be calculated for friendship, for there is little in them that can give pleasure, and no one can spend his days in company with that which is positively painful, or even not pleasant; for it is one of the most obvious tendencies of human nature to avoid the painful and seek the pleasant. Those who get on with one another very fairly, but are not in habits of intimacy, are rather like people having kindly feelings towards one another, than friends; nothing being so characteristic of friends as the living with one another, because the necessitous desire assistance, and the happy, companionship, they being the last persons in the world for solitary existence: but people cannot spend their time together, unless they are mutually pleasant, and take pleasure in the same objects, a quality which is thought to appertain to the friendship of companionship.

**THIS IS THE END OF THE
SIXTH CHAPTER**

CHAPTER VII

THE truest friendship, then, is that which exists between good men, as has already been frequently said. For that it seems is lovable and desirable which is good or pleasant in an absolute sense, but to each individual whatever is such to him; and the friendship of one good man to another rests on both these grounds.

Now affection is like a feeling, but friendship itself is like a moral state: for the former may have for its object even inanimate things, but requital of friendship is attended with moral purpose, which proceeds from a moral state. Again, men wish good to the objects of their friendships for their own sakes, not in the way of a mere feeling, but of moral state.

And the good, in loving their friend, love their own good, as when the good man becomes a friend, he becomes a good to his friend, so

111

that each loves his own good, and repays his friend equally, both in good wishes and pleasure: for equality is said to be a tie of friendship. These points belong most to the friendship between good men.

But between morose, or elderly men, friendship is less apt to arise, because they are somewhat awkward-tempered, and take less pleasure in social intercourse, which seems to be especially characteristic and productive of friendship. So young men become friends quickly, but old men do not, for people do not become friends with any, unless they take pleasure in them; and, in like manner, neither do the morose. Yet men of these classes entertain kindly feelings towards one another: they wish good to one another, and render mutual assistance in respect of their needs, but they are not quite friends, because they neither spend their time together nor take pleasure in one another, which circumstances are thought specially to belong to friendship.

To be a friend to many people, in the way of the perfect friendship, is not possible;

just as you cannot love many persons at once.
It is, so to speak, a state of excess, which
naturally has but one object; and, besides,
it is not an easy thing for a man to be very
much pleased with many people at the same
time, nor perhaps to find many really good
people.   Friendship, too, implies experience
and familiarity, which are very difficult.

But it is possible to please many on the
score of profit or pleasure; for there are
many men of that character, and the services
may be rendered in a very short time.

Of the two imperfect kinds, that which
most resembles the perfect is the friendship
based upon pleasure, in which each renders
the same service to the other, and both take
pleasure in one another, or in the same
objects; such as are the friendships of the
young, for a generous spirit is commoner in
these.   The friendship based on utility is
commercial in character.

Then, again, the happy do not need useful
but pleasant friends, for they wish to have
people to live intimately with; and though
they may for a short time bear with what is

II. H

painful, yet continually no one could endure it, if it were painful to him individually, not even the chief good itself; and so they look out for pleasant friends. Perhaps they ought to require that they should be good also; and good, moreover, to themselves individually, for then they will have all the proper requisites of friendship.

Men in power are often seen to make use of different kinds of friends; for some are useful to them, and others pleasant, but the two qualities are not often found united; for they do not, in fact, seek friends who are both pleasant and virtuous, or who can be useful for noble purposes; but, with a view to attain what is pleasant, they look out for witty men; and again for men who are clever at executing any business put into their hands: and these qualifications are not commonly found united in the same man.

It has been already stated that the good man unites the qualities of pleasantness and usefulness: but then such an one will not be a friend to a superior, unless he be himself superior in virtue; for if this be not the case,

he cannot, being surpassed in one point,
make things equal by a proportionate degree
of friendship.   And characters who unite
superiority of station, and goodness, are not
common.

**THIS IS THE END OF THE
SEVENTH CHAPTER**

CHAPTER VIII

OW all the kinds of friendship which have been already mentioned exist in a state of equality, inasmuch as either the same results accrue to both, and they wish the same things to one another, or else they exchange one thing for another, pleasure, for instance, for profit. It has been said already that friendships of this latter kind are less intense in degree, and less permanent.

And it is their resemblance or dissimilarity to the same thing which makes them to be thought to be and not to be friendships. They look like friendships, in right of their likeness to the friendship which is based on virtue: for the one kind possesses pleasure, the other profit, both of which belong also to true friendship; but, again, they do not look like friendships by reason of their unlikeness to that true kind; which unlikeness consists

116

herein, that while true friendship is above calumny, and so permanent, these quickly change, and differ in many other points.

But there is another form of friendship, that, namely, in which the one party is superior to the other; as between father and son, elder and younger, husband and wife, ruler and ruled. These also differ one from another; for the friendship between parents and children is not the same as between the ruler and the ruled, nor has the father the same towards the son as the son towards the father, nor the husband towards the wife as she towards him; for the function, and therefore the excellence, of each of these is different, and different, therefore, are the causes of their feeling friendship; distinct and different, therefore, are their feelings and states of friendship.

And the same results do not accrue to each from the other, nor, in fact, ought they to be expected: but when children render to their parents what they ought to the authors of their being, and parents on their part render what they ought to their offspring, the friendship between such parties will be permanent and equitable.

But in all friendships which are between superior and inferior, the affection should be in a due proportion; that is, the better man, or the more useful, and so forth, should be the object of a stronger affection than he himself entertains, for when the affection is proportioned to desert, then equality in a certain sense is produced, which seems to be a condition of friendship.

It must be remembered, however, that equality is not the same in justice as in friendship; for, in strict justice, equality in proportion to merit ranks first, and equality as to quantity ranks second, while in friendship this is exactly reversed.

And that equality is thus requisite is plainly seen, when there is a wide difference between two persons in goodness or badness, or prosperity, or something else; for in this case people are not any longer friends, nor do they even expect to be. The clearest illustration is perhaps the case of the gods, because they are most superior in all good things.   It is obvious, too, in the case of kings, for those who are greatly their inferiors do not feel entitled to be friends to them ; nor do very insignificant people expect to be friends to those of very high excellence or wisdom.   Of course, in such cases it is out of the question to attempt to define up to what point they may continue friends; for you may remove many points of agreement and the friendship remain nevertheless ; but when one of the parties is very far separated, as a god from men, it cannot continue any longer.

This has given room for a doubt, whether friends do really wish to their friends the very highest goods, as that they may be gods: for, if the wish were accomplished, they would no longer have them for friends, nor, in fact, would they have the good things they had, because friends are good things. If, then, it has been rightly said that a friend wishes to his friend good things for that friend's sake, it must be understood that he is to remain such as he now is: that is to say, he will wish the greatest good to him, of which, as man, he is capable ; yet perhaps not everything that is good, for every man desires good for himself most of all.

It seems that desire for honour makes most men wish rather to be loved than to love others. For this reason they are fond of flatterers, as a flatterer is an inferior friend, or at least pretends to be so, and to love more than he is loved. But being loved is thought to be nearly the same as being honoured, which most men desire. And yet men seem to choose honour, not for its own sake, but accidentally; for the common run of men delight to be honoured by those in power, because of the hope it raises; that is, they think they will get from them any thing they may happen to be in want of, so they delight in honour as an earnest of future benefit. Those, again, who aspire to gain honour from good men, and from those who are really acquainted with their merits, desire to confirm their own opinion about themselves; so they take pleasure in the conviction that they are good, which is based on the judgment of those who assert it. But men delight in being loved for its own sake, and

so being loved may be judged to be higher
than being honoured, and friendship to be
in itself desirable.　Friendship, moreover, is
thought to consist in loving rather than in
being loved, which is proved by the delight
mothers have in loving their children; for
some give their children to be adopted and
brought up by others, and although they know
them, and love them, never seek to have their
love returned, if it be impossible to have
both; but seem to be content with seeing
their children doing well and loving them,
even though the children, by reason of ignorance, never render to them any filial regard
or love.

Since, then, friendship consists more in
loving than in being loved, and praise is given
to those who are fond of their friends, it
seems that to love is the special virtue of
friends; and so, where love exists in due proportion, people are stable friends, and their
friendship is permanent.　And it is in this
way that they who are unequal may best be
friends, as they may thus be made equal.

Equality, then, and similarity constitute

friendship, and especially the similarity of goodness, for good men, being stable in themselves, are also stable as regards others, and neither ask degrading services, nor render them, but, so to say, rather prevent them : for it is the part of good men neither to do wrong themselves, nor to allow their friends to do it.

Bad men, on the contrary, have no principle of stability : in fact, they do not even continue like themselves; but they become friends for a short time from taking delight in one another's wickedness. Those who are useful or pleasant to one another remain friends for a longer time : so long, that is to say, as they can give one another pleasure or profit.

The friendship based on motives of profit is most of all thought to be formed out of contrary elements : the poor man, for instance, is thus a friend of the rich, and the ignorant, of the man of information ; that is to say, a man desiring that of which he is, as it happens, in want, gives something else in exchange for it. To this same class we may refer the lover and beloved, the beautiful and

the ill-favoured.   For this reason lovers sometimes appear ridiculous, claiming to be the
objects of as intense a feeling as they themselves entertain ; of course, if they are equally
lovable, they are perhaps entitled to claim
this, but if there is nothing lovable about
them, it is ridiculous.

Perhaps, moreover, one opposite does not
desire its opposite for its own sake, but accidentally : the mean is really what is desired ;
it being good for the dry, for instance, not to
become wet, but to arrive at the mean state,
and so with the hot, and with the rest of these
opposites.

However, we may dismiss these questions,
as they are in fact somewhat foreign to our
present purpose.

**THIS IS THE END OF THE
EIGHTH CHAPTER**

IT seems, too, as was stated at the outset, that friendship and justice are concerned with the same objects and exist in the same person; for every community or association, it is thought, involves justice of some kind, and friendship as well. Men address as friends, for instance, those who are their comrades at sea, or in war, and in like manner also those who are brought into association with them in other ways. The friendship, too, is co-extensive with the association, for so also is the justice. This justifies the common proverb, 'the goods of friends are common,' as friendship rests upon association.

Now, brothers and intimate companions have all things in common, but other people have their property separate, and some have more in common, and others less, because the friendships likewise differ in degree. So too do the various principles of justice involved.

They are not the same between parents and children as between brothers, nor between companions as between fellow-citizens merely, and similarly of all the other conceivable friendships. The principles of injustice also are different as regards these different grades, and the acts become greater from being done to friends : for instance, it is worse to rob your companion than one who is merely a fellow-citizen; to refuse help to a brother than to a stranger; and to strike your father than any one else. So then justice naturally increases with the degree of friendship, for they both have the same field, and are equally extensive.

All associations are parts, so to say, of the political association, for in all of them men associate with a view to some advantage, and to procure some of those things which are needful for life. But the political association is thought originally to have been formed and to continue for the sake of some advantage; for this is the point at which legislators aim, affirming that to be just which is generally expedient.

All other associations aim at some parti-

cular advantage; the crew of a vessel, at that
which is to result from the voyage which is
undertaken, with a view to making money, or
some such object; comrades in war, at that
which is to result from the war, grasping either
at wealth or victory, or, it may be, a political
position; and those of the same tribe, in like
manner.

Some associations seem to be formed for
pleasure's sake; those, for instance, of bac-
chanals or club-fellows, which are with a view
to sacrifice, or merely company. But all these
associations are, as it were, subordinate to the
political association; for the aim of the political association is not merely the interest of
the moment, but the interests of our whole
life; with a view to which the members of
it institute sacrifices and their attendant assemblies, to render honour to the gods,
and procure for themselves respite from toil,
combined with pleasure. For it appears that
sacrifices and religious assemblies in old times
were made as a kind of first-fruits after the
ingathering of the crops, because at such
seasons the people had most leisure.

So then it appears that all these associations are parts of the political association, and corresponding friendships will follow upon such associations.

**THIS IS THE END OF THE
NINTH CHAPTER**

CHAPTER X

THERE are three kinds of political constitutions, and an equal number of perverted forms which are, so to say, corruptions of them.

Political constitutions are kingship, aristocracy, and that which recognises the principle of wealth, which it seems appropriate to call timocracy; I give to it the name of a political constitution because people commonly do so. Of these three forms monarchy is the best, and timocracy the worst.

The perversion of monarchy is tyranny, both being monarchies, but widely differing from each other; for the tyrant considers his own advantage, but the king considers the advantage of his subjects. For he is, in fact, not a king, who is not thoroughly independent and superior to the rest in all good things, and he that is this has no further wants: he

128

will not then have to consider his own advantage, but that of his subjects, for he that is not in such a position is a mere king elected by lot for the nonce.

But tyranny is the opposite of kingship, for the tyrant pursues his own good : and of this form of government it is evident that it is the worst of all, and what is worst is the opposite of what is best. Monarchy degenerates into tyranny, for tyranny is a corrupt form of monarchy, that is to say, the bad king becomes a tyrant.

Aristocracy degenerates into oligarchy through the fault of the rulers, in distributing the public property contrary to right proportion, and giving either all that is good, or the greatest share, to themselves; and the offices to the same persons always, making wealth their idol; the result being that a few bear rule, and they bad men in place of the best.

Timocracy degenerates into democracy, for they border closely upon each other; as it is the nature of timocracy to be in the hands of a multitude, and all in the same grade of property are equal. Democracy is the least vicious of all the perverted forms of government, for herein the form of the constitution undergoes least change.

These are generally the changes to which the various constitutions are liable, being the least in degree, and the easiest to make.

Likenesses, and, as it were, models of these constitutions, one may find even in domestic life: for instance, the association of a father with his sons presents the figure of kingship, for the children are the father's care; and hence Homer calls Jupiter father, as kingship is intended to be a paternal rule. Among the Persians, however, the father's rule is tyrannical, for they treat their sons as slaves. The association of master and slave is also tyrannical, for it is the master's interest which is secured by it. Now, this seems to be a right form of tyranny, but the Persian custom seems to be wrong, as different persons require to be governed in different ways.

The association of husband and wife takes the form of aristocracy, for the husband rules by right, and in such points only as the husband should, and gives to the wife all that befits her to have. Where the husband lords it in every thing, he changes the relation into an oligarchy; for he does it contrary to right, and not as being the better of the two. In some instances the wives, being heiresses, take the reins of government: here the rule is carried on, not in right of goodness, but by reason of wealth and power, as it is in oligarchies.

The association of brothers resembles timocracy; for they are equal, except in so far as they differ in age. Hence, if they are very different in age, the friendship ceases to be a fraternal one. Democracy is represented specially by families which have no head, for then all are equal, or in which the head of the family is weak, and so every member of it does that which is right in his own eyes.

**THIS IS THE END OF THE
TENTH CHAPTER**

CHAPTER XI

IN each of these forms of political constitution there seems to be a friendship to the same extent as there is justice. The friendship of a king to his subjects takes the form of superiority in benefaction, for he does good to his subjects if he is a good king, and takes care of their welfare, as a shepherd tends his flock; whence Homer calls Agamemnon, 'shepherd of the people.' And of this same kind is paternal friendship, only that it exceeds the former in the greatness of the benefits done; because the father is the author of being, which seems to be the greatest of all benefits, as well as of maintenance and education. These benefits are also, by the way, ascribed to ancestors generally; and by the law of nature the father has the right of rule over his sons, ancestors over their descendants, and the king over his subjects.

132

These friendships are also between superiors and inferiors, and, on this account, parents are not merely loved, but also honoured. The principle of justice, also, between these parties is not exactly the same, but according to proportion, because so also is the friendship.

The friendship of husband and wife is the same as exists in an aristocracy: for the relation is determined by relative excellence, and the better person has the greater good, and each has what befits: but this is also the rule of justice.

The friendship of brothers is like that of comrades, for they are equal and of like age, and such persons have generally like feelings and like dispositions. Like to this, also, is the friendship in a timocracy; for in a timocracy the citizens wish to be equal and fair, so the government is held in turns and equally; and accordingly their friendship follows the same rule.

In the perverted forms, friendship has as little place as has justice; and least of all in the worst; in a tyranny there is little or no friendship. For, generally, wherever the ruler and the ruled have nothing in common, there is no friendship, for there is no justice. The relation is like that of an artisan to his tools, or of the soul to the body, or of master to servant; all these are benefited by those who use them, but in our relations with inanimate things there is no possibility of friendship or justice, nor, indeed, in our relations to a horse or an ox, or a slave as such, for there is nothing in common; a slave, as such, is an animate tool, a tool an inanimate slave. As a slave, then, friendship between him and his master is impossible, but only as he is a man; for it is thought that there is some principle of justice between every man and every other who can participate in law and contract, and therefore of friendship, in so far as he is man. And so friendships and justice exist only to a small extent in tyrannies, but to a greater extent in democracies, for they who are equal have many things in common.

THIS IS THE END OF THE
ELEVENTH CHAPTER

CHAPTER XII

ALL friendship, then, as has already been stated, implies association; but we may separate from the rest the friendship of kinsmen and that of comrades. The friendships of fellow - citizens, fellow - tribesmen, fellow-sailors, and the like, seem to have more to do with association, for they appear to be based on a sort of compact. We may rank the friendship of hospitality with these.

The friendship of kinsmen is likewise of many kinds, and appears, in all its varieties, to depend on the friendship of parent and child. For parents love their children as being a part of themselves, children love their parents as the source of their being. But parents know their offspring more than the children know that they are sprung from them, and the parent is more closely attached to his offspring than the offspring to the

135

parent; for that which proceeds from a person belongs to that from which it proceeds, as a tooth, or a hair, or any other thing whatever, to its owner: but that from which a thing proceeds does not belong at all to that which proceeds from it, or belongs to it in an inferior degree.

Then, again, length of time makes a considerable difference: for parents love their offspring from the first moment of their being, but children love their parents only after the lapse of time, when they have acquired intelligence or sense. These considerations serve also to show why mothers love their children more than fathers do.

Parents, then, love their children as themselves, for their offspring are, as it were, second selves, which have in virtue of their separation acquired a distinct existence; but children love their parents as being born of them. And brothers love one another from being born of the same parents, for the identity of their relation to their parents constitutes an identity between them; hence come the phrases, 'same blood,' 'same stock'; and so on. In fact, they are in a sense the same, though they are separate individuals.

Then, again, the being brought up together, and the similarity of age, are a great help to friendship, for those of the same age naturally like one another, and persons who sympathise in disposition become comrades, which accounts for the resemblance between the friendship of brothers and the friendship of comrades.

And cousins and all other relatives have the same bond of union to each other, as springing from the same stock; and the strength of this bond varies according to their respective distances from their common ancestor.

The friendship of children for their parents, and of men for the gods, is friendship for something good and above them; for parents are the sources of the greatest possible benefit to children, as to them children owe their existence and nurture and their education from their birth upwards.

Friendship of this kind involves more pleasure and profit than friendship between

strangers, in proportion as their life has more
in common. The friendship of brothers has
all the characteristics of the friendship of comrades and has them in a greater degree if
the brothers are good and generally resemble
one another, inasmuch as brothers are more
closely tied, and from their very birth have
a feeling of affection for one another, and as
there is a greater similarity of disposition
among those who are of the same stock and
are brought up together and educated alike :
and, besides this, they have the greatest opportunities in respect of time for proving
one another, and can therefore depend most
securely upon the test.

Between husband and wife friendship
seems to exist almost as a law of nature, as
man is by nature more disposed to pair than
to form a state ; inasmuch as the family is
prior in order of time to the state, and more
necessary, and procreation is more common
to animals. All the other animals associate
for this purpose only, but human beings live
together, not merely for the sake of procreation,
but also to satisfy the needs of their life in

general. From the very first the functions of the one are distinguished from the functions of the other, and some belong to the man, others to the woman; thus they supply one another's wants, each constituting the common stock.

And for these reasons this sort of friendship is thought to involve both profit and pleasure; it will be also based upon virtue if they are good people; for each of them has his or her proper virtue, and they will both take delight in this quality in each other. Children, too, are thought to be a bond of union between them; hence those who are childless sooner separate, for children are a good which both have in common, and anything in common is a bond of union.

The question how a man is to live with his wife, or, more generally, one friend with another, appears to be no other than this, how it is just for them to live; for plainly justice is not the same thing between one friend and another, as between strangers, or comrades, or mere chance fellow-travellers.

THIS IS THE END OF THE TWELFTH CHAPTER

CHAPTER XIII

THERE are, then, as was stated at the commencement of this book, three kinds of friendship, and in each kind there may be friends on a footing of equality, and friends in the relation of superior and inferior; for people who are equal in goodness may become friends, and a better person may become the friend of a worse; and so too with pleasant people; and also with people who are friends with a view to advantage, as their services may be either equal or unequal. Well, then, those who are equal should in right of this equality each render to the other an equal return of affection, and other friendly offices, and those who are unequal should render a return of affection in proportion to the superiority of the other party.

Fault-finding and blame arise, either solely or most naturally, in friendships of which

utility is the motive; for those whose friendship is based upon virtue, are eager to do
good to one another, as this is a natural
result of virtue and friendship; and between
men who are vying with each other for this
end, there can be no fault-finding or contention: for no one is annoyed at one who
entertains for him the sentiment of friendship
and confers benefits upon him, but, if he
is a man of good feeling, he requites him
with kind actions. And suppose that one
of the two exceeds the other, yet, as he is
attaining his object, he will not find fault
with his friend, for good is the object of
each party.

Neither can there well be quarrels between
men who are friends for pleasure's sake; for
both attain their desire if they delight in living together; but one of them would appear
ridiculous if he should find fault with the
other for not pleasing him, when it is in his
power to forbear intercourse with him. But
the friendship whose motive is utility is very
liable to fault-finding; for as the parties use
one another with a view to advantage, each

always wants the larger share, and thinks he has less than is due, and finds fault with the other for not doing so much as he requires and deserves, though it is impossible for the one who is doing a service to supply all that the other requires.

It seems, also, that as justice is of two kinds, the unwritten and the legal, so the friendship which depends upon utility is of two kinds, either moral or legal. And the most fruitful source of complaints is, that parties contract obligations, and discharge them not in the same line of friendship. The legal friendship is formed upon specified conditions, either purely commercial, on the principle of cash payments, or somewhat more liberal as regards time, but still requiring a definite quid pro quo.

In this legal kind of friendship, the obligation is clear, and admits of no dispute, the friendly element is the delay in requiring its discharge: and, for this reason, in some countries no actions can be maintained at law for the recovery of such debts, it being held that they who have dealt on the footing of credit must be content to abide the issue.

That which may be termed the moral kind of friendship is not formed upon specified conditions, but a man gives as to his friend, and so on; but still he expects to receive an equivalent, or even more, as though he had not given, but lent: he also will complain, if he does not get the obligation discharged in the same way as it was contracted.

Now, this results from the fact that all men, or the generality at least, wish what is noble, but, when tested, choose what is profitable; and, while it is noble to do good disinterestedly, it is profitable to receive a benefit. In such cases one should, if able, make a return proportionate to the good received, and do so willingly, because one ought not to make a disinterested friend of a man against his inclination: one should act, I say, as having made a mistake originally, and received kindness from one from whom one ought not to have received it, he not being a friend, nor doing the act disinterestedly; one should therefore discharge one's self of the obligation, as having received a kindness on specified terms: and the return should be what one would have engaged to pay if able, if one were unable, even the donor would not have expected to be repaid. So that if one is able he ought to repay it. But one ought at first to ascertain from whom one is receiving kindness, and on what understanding, that on that same understanding one may accept or reject it.

It may be questioned whether one is to measure a kindness by the good done to the receiver of it, and make this the standard by which to requite, or whether one is to measure it by the kind intention of the doer.

For they who have received kindnesses frequently plead in depreciation that they have received from their benefactors such things as were small for them to give, or such as they themselves would have got from others: while the doers of the kindnesses affirm that they gave the best they had, and what could not have been got from others, and that it was given in a time of danger, or in such like straits.

May we not say that, as utility is the motive of the friendship, the benefit conferred on the recipient should be taken as the measure, for it is the recipient who requests the kindness, and the other serves him in his need on the understanding that he is to get an equivalent: the assistance rendered is then exactly proportionate to the advantage which the recipient has obtained, and he should therefore repay as much as he gained by it, or even more, this being more creditable.

In friendships based on virtue the question, of course, is never raised, but herein the moral purpose of the benefactor seems to be the proper measure, for virtue and moral character are determined by moral purpose.

**THIS IS THE END OF THE
THIRTEENTH CHAPTER**

II. K

CHAPTER XIV

QUARRELS arise also in those friendships in which the parties are unequal, for each party thinks himself entitled to the larger share, and, of course, when this happens, the friendship is dissolved.

The man who is better than the other thinks that a larger share is his due, as more is always awarded to the good man: and similarly the man who is more profitable to another than that other to him: 'one who is useless,' they say, 'ought not to share equally, for it comes to a tax, and not a friendship, unless the fruits of the friendship are reaped in proportion to the works done': their notion being, that as in a commercial partnership, they who contribute more receive more, so should it be in friendship likewise.

On the other hand, the needy man and the inferior man advance the same claim;

they argue that 'it is the very business of a good friend to help those who are in need, else what is the use of having a good or powerful friend, if one is not to reap any advantage?'

Now each seems to advance a right claim, and to be entitled to get more out of the connection than the other, only not more of the same thing. The superior man should receive more honour, the needy man more profit, as honour is the reward of virtue and beneficence, and money is the means of relieving want.

This is plainly the principle acted upon in political constitutions: he receives no honour who contributes nothing to the common stock; for the property of the public is given to him who promotes the public welfare, and honour is the property of the public. For it is impossible for a person at one and the same time to make money out of the public, and to receive honour from it, as no one is content with the less in every respect. So, they award honour to him who suffers loss as regards money, and money to him whose services can be paid in money: for, as has been stated before, it is the principle of proportion which effects equality and preserves friendship.

The same principles, then, should be observed in the intercourse of friends who are unequal; and to him who benefits another in respect of money, or goodness, that other should repay honour, making requital according to his power; for friendship requires what is possible, not what is strictly due, for this is not possible in all cases, as in the honours paid to the gods and to parents: no man could ever make the due return in these cases, and so he is thought to be a good man who pays respect according to his ability.

For this reason it may be judged never to be allowable for a son to disown his father, whereas a father may his son: because he that owes is bound to pay; now a son can never, by anything he has done, fully requite the benefits first conferred on him by his father, and so is always a debtor. But they to whom anything is owed may cast off their debtors: therefore the father may his son. But at the same time it must perhaps be admitted, that it seems no father ever would sever himself utterly from a son, except in a case of exceeding depravity: for, independently of the natural friendship, it is like human nature not to put away from one's self the assistance which a son might render. But to the son, if he is depraved, assisting his father is a thing to be avoided, or at least one which he will not be very anxious to do; most men being willing enough to receive benefits, but averse to conferring them, as unprofitable.

Let this much suffice on these questions.

THIS IS THE END OF THE
FOURTEENTH CHAPTER

BOOK IX

CHAPTER I

IN all dissimilar friendships it is
the principle of proportion, as has
been already stated, which equal-
ises and preserves the friendship:
just as in a political community
the cobbler gets an equivalent for his shoes
after a certain rate, and the weaver, and all
others in like manner. Now, in this case,
a common measure has been provided by
money, and to this accordingly all things are
referred, and by this are measured. But in
the friendship of love, the complaint is sometimes from the lover that, though he loves
exceedingly, his love is not returned, although
perhaps there is nothing lovable about him:
again, oftentimes from the object of love, that
he who as a suitor promised any and every
thing, now performs nothing. These cases

occur, because the friendship of the lover for
the beloved object is based upon pleasure,
that of the other for him upon utility, and in
one of the parties the requisite quality is not
found. For as these are respectively the
grounds of the friendship, the friendship is
dissolved when the motives to it cease to
exist: the parties loved not one another, but
qualities in one another, which are not permanent, and so neither are the friendships:
whereas the friendship based upon the moral
character of the parties, being independent
and disinterested, is permanent, as we have
already stated before.

Quarrels arise also, when the parties realise
different results, and not those which they
desire; for failing to attain one's special
object is like getting nothing at all. This
may be illustrated by the story of the man
who made promises to a musician, rising in
proportion to the excellence of his music;
but when, the next morning, the musician
claimed the performance of his promises, he
said that he had given him pleasure for
pleasure. Now, if this were what both had

desired, it would have been all right; but if the one desired pleasure, and the other profit, and the one gets his object, but the other does not, the dealing cannot be fair: for a man sets his heart upon what he happens to want, and for the sake of that gives what he does give.

The question then arises, who is to fix the value of the service rendered? the man who first gives, or the man who first receives? for the man who first gives seems to leave it to be fixed by the other party. This, they say, was in fact the practice of Protagoras; when he taught a man any thing, he would bid the learner estimate the worth of the knowledge gained, by his own private opinion; and then he used to take so much from him. In such cases some people adopt the rule, 'With specified reward a friend should be content.'

Those, however, who take the money in advance, and then do nothing of what they said they would do, are rightly censured, their promises having been so far beyond their ability; for such men do not execute what they agreed. The sophists, however, are perhaps obliged to take this course, because no one would give a sixpence for their knowledge. These, then, who do not perform what they have already been paid for doing, are rightly censured.

In cases where no agreement is made about the service rendered, they who disinterestedly render the first service will not raise the question, as we have said before, because it is the nature of friendship based on virtue to be free from such quarrels; the requital is to be made with reference to the intention of the other, the intention being characteristic of the true friend, and of virtue.

And it would seem the same rule should be laid down for those who are connected with one another as teachers and learners of philosophy; for here the value of the commodity cannot be measured by money, and, in fact, an exactly equivalent price cannot be set upon it, but perhaps it is sufficient to do what one can, as in the case of the gods, or one's parents.

But where the original giving is not upon

these terms, but avowedly for some return, the most proper course is perhaps for the requital to be such as both shall deem proportionate; and where this cannot be, it would seem to be not only necessary, but also just, that the recipient should fix the value; for when the first giver gets that which is equivalent to the advantage received by the other, or to what he would have given to secure the pleasure he has had, then he has the value from him. For this is the course adopted in matters of buying and selling, and in some states, indeed, the law does not allow of actions arising out of voluntary contracts; on the principle that when one man has trusted another, he must be content to have the obligation discharged in the same spirit as he originally contracted it, that is to say, it is thought fairer for the trusted, than for the trusting, party, to fix the value. For, in general, those who have and those who wish to get things, do not set the same value on them: what belongs to us, and what we give away, appears to each of us to be worth a great deal. Nevertheless, the return to be

made must be fixed according to the estimate
of the receiver; it should perhaps be added,
that the receiver should estimate what he
has received, not by the value he sets upon
it now that he actually has it, but by the
value which he set upon it before he obtained it.

**THIS IS THE END OF THE
FIRST CHAPTER**

CHAPTER II

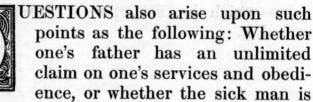UESTIONS also arise upon such points as the following: Whether one's father has an unlimited claim on one's services and obedience, or whether the sick man is to obey his physician? or whether, in an election of a general, the warlike qualities of the candidates should be alone regarded?

Similarly, whether one ought to do a service to one's friend rather than to a good man, and requite a benefactor rather than make a present to a comrade, supposing that both are not within one's power?

It is no easy task to determine all such questions precisely, inasmuch as they involve numerous differences of all kinds, in respect of amount, and what is honourable, and what is necessary. It is obvious, of course, that one must not bestow everything that one has upon the same person. As a general rule, the requital of benefits is a higher duty than conferring favours on one's comrade; in other words, the discharging of a debt is more obligatory upon one than the duty of giving to a comrade. And yet this rule may admit of exceptions; for instance, if a man has been ransomed from the hands of brigands, ought he in turn to ransom his ransomer, whoever he may be, or to repay him on his demand, even though he has not been taken prisoner, rather than ransom his own father? For it would seem, that a man ought to ransom his father, even in preference to himself.

Well, then, as has been said already, as a general rule the debt should be discharged, but if in a particular case giving instead of repaying is more noble or necessary, we must be swayed by these considerations. For in some cases it is not even fair to repay the original service, for instance, when the original benefactor has conferred a kindness on a good man, knowing him to be such, whereas this said good man has to repay it, believing him to be a scoundrel.

And, again, in certain cases no obligation lies on a man to lend to one who has lent to him; suppose, for instance, that a bad man lent to him, as being a good man, under the notion that he should get repaid, whereas the said good man has no hope of repayment from him, being a bad man. If, then, this is the true state of the case, the claim is not equal, or if this is not the true state of the case, though the parties think it to be so; in so acting, people are not to be thought to act wrongly. In short, as has been often-times stated before, all statements concerning the feelings and actions of men can be definite only in proportion as their object-matter is so; it is, of course, quite obvious that all people have not the same claim upon one; nor are the claims of one's father unlimited; just as Jupiter does not claim all kinds of sacrifice without distinction; and as the claims of parents, brothers, comrades, and benefactors, are all different, we must give to each what belongs to and befits each.

And this is seen to be the course commonly pursued: to a wedding men commonly invite their relatives, for they have a share in the family, and therefore in all the acts in any way pertaining thereto : and at funerals men think that relatives ought to assemble in preference to other people, for the same reason.

And it would seem that, in respect of maintenance, it is our duty to assist our parents in preference to all others, as being their debtors, and because it is more honourable to assist the authors of our existence in that respect, than ourselves. We ought, likewise, to pay honour to our parents just as to the gods, but not every kind of honour: the same honour, for instance, is not due to a father as to a mother : nor, again, is the same honour due to a father as to a wise man or a general, but that which is due to a father; and, in like manner, to a mother that which is due to a mother.

To all our elders, also, we ought to pay the honour befitting their age, by rising up in their presence, giving them the place of honour at the table, and all similar marks of respect. To our comrades and brothers, on the other hand, we should give freedom of speech and free participation in all we have. And to kinsfolk and fellow-tribesmen, and fellow-citizens, and all other persons, we should constantly try to render their due, and to discriminate what belongs to each in respect of nearness of connection, or goodness, or intimacy: of course, in the case of those of the same class, the discrimination is easier; in that of those who are in different classes, it is a matter of more trouble. This, however, should not be a reason for giving up the attempt, but we must observe the distinctions so far as it is practicable to do so.

THIS IS THE END OF THE SECOND CHAPTER

NOTHER difficult question is, whether we ought, or ought not, to dissolve friendships with those whose character is no longer such as it was originally.

Surely, in respect of those whose motive to friendship is utility or pleasure, there can be nothing wrong in dissolving the friendship, when they no longer possess those qualities; for they were friends, not of one another, but of those qualities; and these having failed, it is only reasonable to expect that they should cease to entertain the sentiment.

But a man has fair ground for complaint if another, being really attached to him because of advantage or pleasure, pretended to be so because of his moral character; in fact, as we said at the commencement, the most common source of quarrels between friends is their not being friends on the same grounds, as they suppose themselves to be.

If, then, a man deceives himself, and supposes that he is beloved for his moral character, though the other's conduct gives no ground for such an idea, he has but himself to blame; but if he is deceived by the pretence of the other, he has fair ground for complaint against the man who has so deceived him, even more than against utterers of false coin, inasmuch as the wrong affects a more precious object.

But if a man admits another to his friendship as a good man, who turns out, and is found by him, to be a scoundrel, is he still to love him? or may we not say at once it is impossible, as it is not every thing which is lovable, but only that which is good. A bad man is not lovable and ought not to be loved; for we ought not to be lovers of evil, nor make ourselves like what is base; which would be implied, because we have said before, like is friendly to like.

Ought the friendship, then, to be immediately broken off? Perhaps not in all cases; but only in the case of those who are incurably depraved; when there is a chance of amendment, we are bound to aid in repairing the moral character of our friends, even more than their substance, inasmuch as it is better and more closely related to friendship. Still, he who should break off the friendship is not to be judged to act wrongly, for he never was a friend to such a character as the other now is, and, therefore, since the man is changed, and he cannot reduce him to his original state, he withdraws his friendship.

But suppose that one party remains what he was when the friendship was formed, while the other becomes morally improved, and widely different from his friend in virtue; is the improved character to treat the other as a friend?

May we not say it is impossible? The case, of course, is clearest where there is a great difference, as in the friendship of boys: for suppose that of two boyish friends, the one still remains a boy in mind, while the other has become a man of the highest character, how can they be friends, when they no longer are pleased with the same objects, nor like and dislike the same things? For they can no longer feel sympathy with one another, and without sympathy, as we saw, they cannot be friends, since they cannot live together. But this is a point which has been already discussed.

Ought, then, a man, in cases of this sort, to behave towards his former friend exactly as he would behave to him had their friendship never existed?

Surely he ought to bear in mind the intimacy of past times, and just as we think ourselves bound to do favours for our friends in preference to strangers, so to those who have been friends and are so no longer, we should show some consideration for the sake of past friendship, unless the cause of severance is excessive wickedness on their part.

**THIS IS THE END OF THE
THIRD CHAPTER**

CHAPTER IV

RIENDLY relations to others, and
the characteristics by which we
define friendship, seem to be derived from our relations to ourselves.

For a friend may be defined as one who
wishes and does what is good, or what he
believes to be good, to another for that other's
sake; or as one who wishes his friend to
exist and to live for that friend's own sake.
This is the feeling of mothers towards their
children, and of friends who have had a
quarrel. Others define a friend as one who
lives with another and chooses the same objects, or as one who sympathises with another
in his sorrows and in his joys; this too is
especially the case with mothers.

By some one of these characteristics people
generally define friendship: and every one
of these characteristics is found in the re-

lation of the good man to himself, and in the relation of all other men to themselves in so far as they suppose themselves to be good. For, as has been said before, virtue and the good man seem to be the measure of everything.

For the good man is at one with himself, and desires the same things with every part of his soul, and wishes for himself both what is, and what seems good, and does that, as it is characteristic of the good man to work out that which is good, for his own sake; that is to say, for the sake of the rational part of him, which is generally thought to be a man's self. Also, he wishes that he may live and be preserved, and especially that his reason may live, for existence is a good to him that is a good man.

But it is for himself that each individual wishes what is good, and no man would choose to have all that is good on condition that he should be other than he now is. God, indeed, now possesses the supreme good, but only in virtue of being what He is. And a man's reason would seem to be his self, or at least to be so in a truer sense than anything else is.

Such a man wishes to live with himself; for his own company is pleasant to him. The memories of his past actions are full of delight, and his hopes for the future are good, and such hopes are pleasant. His mind, too, is well stored with matter for contemplation, and he most especially sympathises with himself in sorrow and joy, for the objects which give him pain and pleasure are at all times the same, and not one thing to-day, and a different one to-morrow; for he is, so to speak, not given to change his mind. Since all these characteristics mark the good man's relations to himself, and since his relations to his friend are the same as his relations to himself—for his friend is a second self—friendship may be defined by means of one or other of these characteristics, and friends may be said to be persons in whom these characteristics are found. Whether it is possible or not for a man to be a friend of himself, is a question we will not at present entertain. It would seem to be possible, in so far as two or more of the specified conditions are satisfied, and because the highest

degree of friendship, in the usual acceptation
of that term, resembles the feeling entertained
by a man towards himself.

But the characteristics we have mentioned
are to all appearance found in the generality
of men, even though they are bad men.

Perhaps, therefore, we may conclude that
such persons share them in so far as they
are satisfied with themselves, and suppose
themselves to be good, for they are not either
really, or even apparently, found in anyone
who is utterly worthless and impious, and we
may almost say that they are not found even
in those who are bad men at all. For such
men are at variance with themselves, and
lust after different things from those which
in cool reason they wish for, as the incontinent do; for instance, they choose things
which, though injurious, are pleasant, in preference to those which in their own minds
they believe to be good. Others again, from
cowardice and indolence, abstain from doing
what they think is best for themselves; while
those whose depravity has led them to com-
mit many dreadful crimes, hate and avoid

life, and accordingly kill themselves. The
wicked, moreover, seek others in whose
company to spend their time, and try to
escape from themselves, for when they are
alone they have many unpleasant subjects of
memory, and can only anticipate others of
the same kind, but when they are in the
company of others they forget them. There
is nothing lovable in them, and so they have
no friendly feelings towards themselves.

Neither, in fact, can such people sympathise
with themselves in joy or sorrow; for their soul
is, as it were, torn by faction, one part of it,
by reason of its viciousness, feeling pain at
having to abstain from certain things, another
part feeling pleasure; and the one drags them
this way, and the other that way, as though
actually tearing them asunder. And though
it is impossible actually to have at the same
time the sensations of pain and pleasure; yet
after a little time, the wicked man is pained
at having been pleased, and he wishes that
he had not enjoyed such pleasures; for the
wicked are full of regrets.

It is plain, then, that the wicked man

cannot be in the position of a friend even towards himself, for he has in himself nothing which can excite the sentiment of friendship. If then to be in this condition is utterly miserable, it is a man's duty to flee from wickedness with all his might, and to strive to be good, for thus may he be friends with himself, and may come to be a friend to another.

THIS IS THE END OF THE
FOURTH CHAPTER

CHAPTER V

GOODWILL resembles friendship, but it is not identical with it, for goodwill may be felt towards people whom we do not know, and who are not aware that we wish them well, but friendship cannot. This, by the way, has been said before. And, further, goodwill is not the same as affection, for it does not imply intensity nor yearning, which are both consequences of affection. Affection moreover implies intimacy, but goodwill may arise quite suddenly, as when we feel goodwill towards competitors in the public games. We wish them well, and sympathise with them, but we should not do anything to help them, for, as we said, we conceive this feeling of kindness suddenly, and so have but a superficial liking.

It seems then to be the beginning of friendship; as pleasure in the sight of a person is

171

the commencement of love : for no one falls
in love without being first pleased with the
personal appearance of the beloved object;
and yet he who takes pleasure in it does not
therefore necessarily love, but when he wearies
for the object in its absence, and desires its
presence. Exactly in the same way, men
cannot be friends without having passed
through the stage of goodwill, and yet they
who are in that stage do not necessarily
advance to friendship : they merely have an
inert wish for the good of those toward whom
they entertain the feeling, but would not help
them in any action, nor put themselves out of
the way for them. So that, in a metaphorical
way of speaking, one might say that goodwill
is dormant friendship, and when it has
endured for a space, and ripened into intimacy, becomes real friendship ; but not that
friendship whose motive is advantage or
pleasure, for such motives cannot produce
even goodwill.

He who has received a kindness requites
it by goodwill towards his benefactor, and is
right in so doing : but he who wishes another

to be prosperous, because he has hope of advantage through his instrumentality, does not seem to be kindly disposed to that person, but rather to himself; just as neither is he his friend if he pays court to him for any interested purpose.

Goodwill always arises by reason of goodness and a certain amiability, as when one man gives another the notion of being noble or brave, and so on, as we said in the case of competitors in the public games.

THIS IS THE END OF THE
FIFTH CHAPTER

CHAPTER VI

NANIMITY also appears to be an element in friendship, and therefore is not the same as agreement in opinion, as this might exist even between people unacquainted with one another.

Nor do we call people who agree in opinion on any subject, as, for instance, on astronomy, unanimous, for unanimity on matters of this kind has no element of friendship, but we say that states are unanimous when they agree respecting points of expediency, and take the same line, and carry out what has been determined in common consultation.

Thus we see that it is with regard to practical matters that people are said to be unanimous, and especially with regard to matters of importance, and things that may be shared by both or all the persons concerned. For instance, a state is unanimous

when all the citizens are agreed that the
magistrates should be elected, or that an
alliance should be formed with the Lacedæmonians, or that Pittacus should be appointed
ruler, that is to say, supposing he himself was
willing.　But when each wishes himself to be
in power, as the brothers in the Phœnissæ,
they quarrel and form parties; for, plainly,
unanimity does not merely imply that both
parties entertain the same idea whatever it
may be, but that they do so in respect of the
same object, as when both the populace and
the sensible men of a state desire that the
best men should be in office, for then all attain
their object.

Unanimity, then, seems to be political
friendship, as indeed it is said to be: for it
has to do with the interests and concerns of
life.

And this is the kind of unanimity that
exists between good men; for they are of one
mind both with themselves and with others,
standing, so to speak, on the same ground.
The wishes of such men are stable, and do not
ebb and flow like the Euripus, and they wish

what is just and expedient, and unite their efforts to attain it.

Bad men, on the contrary, cannot be unanimous any more than they can be friends, except to a very slight extent; as they desire an unfair share of all things profitable, and seek to avoid their share of labour and service for the common good; and while each man wishes for these things for himself, he is jealous of and hinders his neighbour; for if they do not watch over the common good, it is lost. The result is that they quarrel, trying to force one another to do what is right, but unwilling to do it themselves.

THIS IS THE END OF THE

SIXTH CHAPTER

ENEFACTORS seem to love those whom they have benefited more than those who have received benefits love their benefactors, and as this appears contrary to reason, people seek for some explanation.

The account of the matter which satisfies most persons is that the latter are debtors, and the former creditors; and therefore that, as in the case of actual loans, the debtors wish their creditors out of the way, while the creditors are anxious for the preservation of their debtors, so benefactors desire the continued existence of those whom they have benefited, in the hope of receiving favours in return, while the debtors are not particularly anxious to repay.

Epicharmus would very probably say, that those who give this explanation take too low a view of human nature; yet it appears to be true to life, for the generality of men have short memories on these points, and are more eager to receive benefits than to confer them.

But the real cause, it would seem, is something that lies deeper in the nature of things, and the case is not parallel to that of creditors; for creditors have no affection for their debtors, but merely a wish for their preservation in order that they may repay: whereas, in point of fact, those who have conferred benefits, feel friendship and love for those whom they have benefited, even though they neither are, nor can by possibility hereafter be, in a position to do them any service.

And this is the case also with artisans; every one, I mean, feels more affection for his own work, than that work possibly could for him, if it were animate. It is perhaps specially the case with poets: for these entertain very great affection for their poems, loving them as their own children. It is to this kind of thing I should be inclined to compare the case of benefactors; for the object of their kindness is their own work, and so they love this more than this does its creator.

And the reason of this is, that we all
desire and love existence; but we exist
by acts of working, that is, by living and
acting: he then who has created a given work
exists, it may be said, by his act of working:
therefore he loves his work, because he loves
existence. And this is natural, for the work
produced displays in act what existed before
potentially.

Then again, the benefactor has a sense of
honour in right of his action, so that he may
well take pleasure in him in whom this resides; but to him who has received the benefit, there is nothing honourable in respect of
his benefactor, only something useful, which
is both less pleasant and less lovable.

Again, pleasure is derived from the actual
working out of a present action, from the
anticipation of a future one, and from the
recollection of a past one: but the highest
pleasure and special object of affection is that
which attends on the actual working. Now
the benefactor's work abides, for that which
is noble is enduring, but the advantage of
him who has received the benefit passes away.

Again, there is pleasure in recollecting noble actions, but in recollecting advantageous ones, there is none at all, or much less : by the way though, the contrary is true of the expectation of advantage.

Further, the feeling of affection is like doing something; but being loved, is like having something done to one.

So then, love and feelings of friendship attend on those who, in the given case of a benefaction, are the superior party.

Once more : all people value most what has cost them much labour in the production; for instance, people who have themselves made their money, are fonder of it than those who have inherited it: and receiving a benefit, involves no labour, but conferring it, is a matter of trouble.   And this is the reason why mothers are most fond of their offspring; for their part in producing them is attended with most labour, and they know more certainly that they are their own.   This feeling would seem also to belong to benefactors.

**THIS IS THE END OF THE
SEVENTH CHAPTER**

QUESTION is also raised as to whether it is right to love one's self best, or some one else : because men find fault with those who love themselves best, and call them in a disparaging way lovers of self; and the bad man is thought to do every thing he does for his own sake merely, and the more so the more depraved he is; accordingly, men reproach him with never doing any thing unselfish : whereas the good man acts from a sense of honour (and the more so the better man he is), and for his friend's sake, and is careless of his own interest.

But with these theories facts are at variance, and not unnaturally; for it is commonly said also that a man ought to love most him who is most his friend, and he is most a friend who wishes good to him to whom he wishes it for that man's sake, even though

no one knows. Now these conditions, and
in fact all the rest by which a friend is
characterised, belong specially to each individual in respect of himself: for we have
said before that all the friendly feelings to
others are derived from those which have
self primarily for their object. And all the
current proverbs support this view; for instance, 'one soul,' 'the goods of friends are
common,' 'equality is a tie of friendship,'
'the knee is nearer than the shin.' For all
these things exist specially with reference to
a man's own self: he is specially a friend to
himself, and so he is bound to love himself
the most.

It is with good reason questioned, which
of the two parties one should follow, both
having plausibility on their side. Perhaps
then, in respect of theories of this kind, the
proper course is to distinguish and define
how far, and in what way, each is true. If
we could ascertain the sense in which each
uses the term 'self loving,' this point might
be cleared up.

Well now, they who use it disparagingly

give the name to those who, in respect of wealth, and honours, and pleasures of the body, give to themselves the larger share: because the mass of mankind grasp after these, and are earnest about them as being the best things; which is the reason why they are matters of contention. They who are covetous in regard to these, gratify their lusts and passions in general, that is to say, the irrational part of their soul: but the mass of mankind are covetous, for which reason the appellation has taken its rise from that mass which is low and bad. Of course they who are self-loving in this sense are justly reproached.

And it is quite plain that the generality of men are accustomed to apply the term to denominate those who do give such things to themselves: suppose, for instance, that a man were anxious to do, more than other men, acts of justice, or temperance, or any other virtuous acts, and, in general, were to secure to himself that which is abstractedly noble and honourable, no one would call him self-loving, nor blame him.

Yet such an one might be judged to be more truly self-loving: certainly he gives to himself the things which are most noble and most good, and gratifies that principle of his nature which is most rightfully authoritative, and obeys it in every thing: and just as that which possesses the highest authority is thought to constitute a state or any other system, so also in the case of a man: and so he is most truly self-loving who loves and gratifies this principle.

Again, men are said to be continent or incontinent, according as reason rules within them or not, it being plainly implied thereby, that it is the reason which constitutes each individual; and people are thought to have done of themselves, and voluntarily, those things specially which are done with reason.

It is plain, therefore, that this principle does, either entirely or specially, constitute the individual man, and that the good man specially loves this. For this reason then he must be specially self-loving in another sense than that which is reproached, and as

far superior to it, as living in accordance
with reason is to living at the beck and call
of passion, and aiming at the truly noble to
aiming at apparent advantage.

Now all approve and commend those who
are eminently earnest about noble actions,
and if all would vie with one another in
respect of what is noble, and be intent upon
doing what is most truly noble and honourable, society at large would have all that is
proper, while each individual in particular
would have the greatest of goods, virtue
being assumed to be such.

And so the good man ought to be self-
loving : because by doing what is noble he
will benefit himself, and do good to others :
but the bad man ought not to be, because
he will harm himself and his neighbours by
following low and evil passions. In the case
of the bad man, what he ought to do and
what he does are at variance, but the good
man does what he ought to do, for reason
always chooses what is best for itself, and the
good man puts himself under the direction of
reason.

It is true likewise of the good man, that he does many things for the sake of his friends and his country, even to the extent of dying for them, if need be: for he will throw away money, and honours, and, in short, all the good things which others fight for, claiming for himself that which is noble. And he will prefer a brief and great joy to a tame and enduring one, and to live nobly for one year, than ordinarily for many, and one great and noble action to many trifling ones. And this is perhaps that which befalls men who die for their country and friends: they choose great glory for themselves; and they will lavish their own money, that their friends may receive more, for hereby the friend gets the money, but the man himself that which is noble; so, in fact, he gives to himself the greater good. It is the same with honours and offices; all these things he will give up to his friend, because this reflects honour and praise on himself: and so with good reason is he esteemed a fine character, since he chooses what is noble before all things else. It is possible also to give up the opportunities of action to a friend; and to have caused a friend's doing a thing may be more noble than having done it one's self.

In short, in all praiseworthy things the good man does plainly give to himself a larger share of what is noble. In this sense it is right to be self-loving, in the vulgar acceptation of the term it is not.

THIS IS THE END OF THE EIGHTH CHAPTER

QUESTION is raised also respecting the happy man, whether he will need friends, or not?

Some say, that those who are blessed and independent have no need of friends, for they already have all that is good, and so, as being independent, want nothing further; whereas the notion of a friend's office is to be as it were a second self, and procure for a man what he cannot get by himself: hence the saying, 'When fortune gives us good, what need we friends?'

On the other hand, it looks absurd while we are assigning to the happy man all other good things, not to give him friends, which are, after all, thought to be the greatest of external goods.

Again, if it is more characteristic of a friend to confer, than to receive, benefits, and if to be beneficent belongs to the good man and to the character of virtue, and if it is more noble to confer benefits on friends than strangers, the good man will need friends to receive benefits from him. And out of this last consideration springs a question, whether the need of friends be greater in prosperity or adversity, since the unfortunate man wants some one to help him, and they who are fortunate want some one whom they may help.

Again, it is perhaps absurd to make our happy man a solitary being, for no man would choose the possession of all goods in the world on the condition of solitariness, man being a social animal, and formed by nature for living with others: of course, the happy man has this qualification, since he has all those things which are good by nature: and it is obvious, that the society of friends and good men must be preferable to that of strangers and ordinary people, and we conclude, therefore, that the happy man does need friends.

But then, what do they mean whom we quoted first, and how are they right? Is it not that the mass of mankind mean by friends those who are useful ? and, of course, the happy man will not need such, because he has all good things already; neither will he need such as are friends with a view to the pleasurable, or at least only to a slight extent; because his life, being already pleasant, does not want pleasure imported from without: and so, since the happy man does not need friends of these kinds, he is thought not to need any at all.

But it may be, this is not true: for it was stated originally, that happiness is a form of activity; and it is clear that an activity is something that must come into being, and does not already exist like a mere piece of property.

If, then, as we said at the commencement, happiness consists in life and activity, and the activity of the good man is in itself good and pleasant, and if the sense that a thing is our own is pleasant, and if we can view our neighbours better than ourselves, and their actions better than we can our own, then the actions of good men who are his friends, give pleasure to the good man; inasmuch as they have both the requisites which are naturally pleasant. So the man in the highest state of happiness will need friends of this kind, since he desires to contemplate good actions, and actions of his own, which those of his friend, being a good man, are.

Again, common opinion requires that the happy man must have a pleasant life: now life is burdensome to a man in solitude, for it is not easy to work continuously by one's self, but in company with, and in regard to others, it is easy, and therefore the activity, being pleasant in itself, will be more continuous. This ought to be the case with the happy man; for the good man, in that he is good, takes pleasure in the actions which accord with virtue, and is annoyed at those which spring from vice, just as a musical man is pleased with beautiful melodies, and annoyed by bad ones. And besides, as Theognis says, virtue itself may be improved by practice, from living with the good.

But if we look deeper into the nature of

things, it will probably appear that a good
friend is naturally desirable to the good man.
We have said before, that whatever is naturally good, is also in itself good and pleasant
to the good man; now life is defined, in the
case of animals, by the power of feeling, in
the case of man, by the power of feeling or
thought; but a faculty realises itself in activity, and it is upon the activity that the faculty
essentially depends; so that life seems mainly
to consist of thought and perception. Now
life is in itself one of the things that are
good and pleasant, for it possesses the de-
finiteness which is of the nature of the good,
but that which is naturally good is good to
the good man: for which reason life seems
to be pleasant to all men. Of course this
must not be held to apply to a life which
is depraved and corrupted, or one spent in
pain, for such a life is indefinite, as are its
inherent qualities. However, what is to be
said of pain, will be clearer in what is to
follow.

Life, then, is in itself good and pleasant,
as appears also from the fact that all desire

it, and specially those who are good and truly happy; for life is most desirable to them, and their life is the most blessed. But he who sees perceives that he sees, and he who hears perceives that he hears; and in all the other instances, in like manner, there is a faculty which reflects upon and perceives that we exercise the activity, so that we can perceive that we perceive, and understand that we understand. But to be thus conscious of thought and perception is to be conscious of existence, for existence was defined to be perceiving or thinking. Now to perceive that one lives is a thing pleasant in itself, life being a thing naturally good, and the perceiving of the presence in ourselves of things naturally good, being pleasant.

Therefore, life is desirable, and to the good specially so, since existence is good and pleasant to them; for they receive pleasure from the internal consciousness of that which in itself is good.

But the good man stands in the same relation to his friend as to himself, for his friend is a second self; therefore as his own

II. N

existence is desirable to each, so too or similarly at least, is his friend's existence. But we saw that existence is desirable because of the consciousness that one's self is good, such a consciousness being in itself pleasant. Therefore one ought to be thoroughly conscious of one's friend's existence, which will result from living with him, that is, sharing in his words and thoughts: for this is the meaning of the term as applied to the human species, not merely feeding together, as in the case of beasts.

If then to the truly happy man existence is in itself desirable, being naturally good and pleasant, and if a friend's existence is much the same to him as his own, then a friend also must be a desirable thing. But that which is desirable a man ought to have, or else he will be in this point deficient. The conclusion therefore is that if a man is to be happy, he will need good friends.

THIS IS THE END OF THE NINTH CHAPTER

CHAPTER X

RE we then to make our friends as numerous as possible? or, as in respect of acquaintance it is thought to have been well said, 'have not thou many acquaintances, yet be not without'; so too in respect of friendship may we adopt the precept, and say, that a man should not be without friends, nor again have exceeding many friends?

Now, as for friends who are chosen with a view to being useful, the maxim I have quoted will, it seems, fit in exceedingly well, because to requite the services of many is a matter of labour, and a whole life would not be long enough to do this for them. So that a larger number of such friends than are sufficient for one's own life would be superfluous, and a hindrance to noble living; and so we do not want many friends of this kind. And again, of those who are chosen with a view to

195

pleasure, a few are quite enough, as a little sweetening is enough in our food.

But of good friends, are we to make as many as ever we can, or is there to be any limit to the number of our friends, as there is in a state? For you cannot make a state out of ten men, and if you had a hundred thousand, a state would cease to be a state. However, the number of citizens is not perhaps some one definite number, but any between certain extreme limits.

Well, of friends likewise there is a limited number, which perhaps may be laid down to be the greatest number with whom it would be possible to keep up intimacy; this being thought to be one of the greatest marks of friendship, and it being quite obvious that it is not possible to be intimate with many, in other words, to part one's self among many. And besides it must be remembered, that a man's friends are also to be friends with one another, if they are all to live together; but this is a matter of difficulty with a large number.

It comes likewise to be difficult to bring home to one's self the joys and sorrows of many; for in all probability one would have to sympathise at the same time with the joys of this one, and the sorrows of that other.

Perhaps then it is well not to endeavour to have very many friends, but so many as are enough for intimacy; because, in fact, it would seem to be impossible to be very much a friend to many at the same time. And for the same reason, it is impossible to be in love with many persons at the same time; for love is a kind of excessive friendship, which implies but one object: and all strong emotions must be limited in the number towards whom they are felt.

And if we look to facts, this seems to be so; for we do not find a number of people bound together by the kind of friendship that exists between comrades, all the famous friendships of the kind having been between two persons. Whereas those who have many friends, and meet everybody on the footing of intimacy, seem to be friends really to no one, except in the way of general society; I mean, the characters denominated as over-complaisant.

To be sure, in the way merely of society, a man may be a friend to many without being necessarily over-complaisant, but being truly good; but one cannot be a friend to many, because of their virtue, and for the person's own sake; in fact, it is a matter for contentment to find even a few such.

**THIS IS THE END OF THE
TENTH CHAPTER**

CHAPTER XI

AGAIN : are friends most needed in prosperity or in adversity? They are required, we know, in both states, because the unfortunate need help, and the prosperous want people to live with and to do kindnesses to: for they have a desire to act kindly to some one.

To have friends is more necessary in adversity, and therefore in this case useful ones are wanted; and to have them in prosperity is more noble, and this is why the prosperous want good men for friends, it being preferable to confer benefits on, and to live with, these. For the very presence of friends is pleasant even in adversity; since men when grieved are comforted by the sympathy of their friends.

And from this, by the way, the question might be raised, whether it is that they do in a manner take part of the weight of calamities,

199

or only that their presence being pleasurable, and the consciousness of their sympathy, make the pain of the sufferer less.

However, we will not further discuss whether these which have been suggested or some other causes produce the relief, at least the effect we speak of is a matter of plain fact.

But their presence has probably a mixed effect. On the one hand, the mere sight of friends is pleasant, especially to one in misfortune, and actual help towards lessening the grief is afforded; for a friend, if he is gifted with tact, can do much to comfort by look and word, because he is well acquainted with the sufferer's temper and disposition, and therefore knows what things give him pleasure and pain. But on the other hand, the perceiving a friend to be grieved at his misfortunes causes the sufferer pain, because every one avoids being a cause of pain to his friends. And for this reason they who are of a manly nature are cautious not to involve their friends in their pain; and unless a man is exceedingly callous to the pain of others, he cannot bear the pain which is thus caused to his friends; in short, he does not allow others to lament with him, not being given to lamentations himself : women, it is true, and effeminate men, like to have others to groan with them, and love such as friends and sympathisers. But it is plain that it is our duty in all things to imitate the highest character.

On the other hand, the advantages of friends in our prosperity are, the pleasurable intercourse, and the consciousness that they are pleased at our good fortune.

It would seem, therefore, that we ought to call in friends readily on occasion of good fortune, because it is noble to be ready to do good to others : but on occasion of bad fortune, we should do so with reluctance; for we should as little as possible make others share in our ills, on which principle goes the saying, 'I am unfortunate, let that suffice.' The most proper occasion for calling them in is, when with small trouble or annoyance to themselves they can be of very great use to the person who needs them.

But, on the contrary, it is fitting perhaps to go to one's friends when they are in trouble, unasked and with alacrity; for kindness is a friend's office, and specially towards those who are in need, and who do not demand it as a right, this being more creditable and more pleasant to both, but, when they are in prosperity, to go readily, if we can aid them in their good fortune, as this is one of the uses of a friend, but to be backward in sharing it, any great eagerness to receive advantage not being noble.

One should perhaps be careful not to appear ungracious in declining the sympathy or help of friends, for this happens occasionally.

It appears then, that the presence of friends is, under all circumstances, desirable.

THIS IS THE END OF THE ELEVENTH CHAPTER

ARISTOTLE

CHAPTER XII

AY we not say then, that as lovers delight above all things in the sight of each other, and choose the sense of sight rather than any of the others, because love 'is engendered in the eyes, with gazing fed,' in like manner there is nothing which friends desire so much as living together, for the essence of friendship is community. Again, a man stands in the same relation to his friend as to himself; but with regard to himself, the consciousness of existence is desirable, so too then is that with regard to his friend.

And besides, the activity of friends is realised in living together, and so with good reason they desire this. And whatever in each man's opinion constitutes existence, or whatsoever it is for the sake of which they choose life, herein they wish their friends to join with them, and so some men drink together, others gamble, others join in gymnastic exercises or hunting, others study philosophy together; in each case spending their days together in that which they like best of all things in life, for as they wish to be intimate with their friends, they do and partake in those things whereby they think to attain this object.

Therefore the friendship of the wicked comes to be depraved; for being unstable, they share in what is bad, and become depraved in being made like to one another: but the friendship of the good is good, growing with their intercourse; they improve also, as it seems, by repeated acts, and by mutual correction, for they receive impress from one another in the points which give them pleasure; whence the saying, 'Thou from the good, good things shalt surely learn.'

Here then we will terminate our discussion of friendship. The next thing is to discuss pleasure.

THIS IS THE END OF THE TWELFTH CHAPTER

BOOK X

CHAPTER I

NEXT, it would seem natural to discuss pleasure, for it is thought to be most closely bound up with our nature; and so men train the young, guiding them on their course by the rudders of pleasure and pain. And to like and dislike what one ought, is judged to be most important for the formation of good moral character; because these feelings extend all one's life through, giving a bias towards, and exerting an influence on the side of, virtue and happiness, since men choose what is pleasant, and avoid what is painful.

Subjects such as these then, it would seem, we ought by no means to pass by, and specially since they involve much difference of opinion. There are those who say that pleasure is the chief good; there are others, who on the contrary maintain that it is exceedingly bad; some perhaps from a real conviction that such is the case, others from a notion that it is better, in reference to our life and conduct, to represent pleasure as bad, even if it is not so really; arguing, that as the mass of men have a bias towards it, and are the slaves of their pleasures, it is right to draw them to the opposite extreme, for that so they may possibly arrive at the mean.

I confess, I suspect the soundness of this policy; in matters relating to men's feelings and actions, theories are less convincing than facts: whenever, therefore, they are found conflicting with actual experience, they not only are despised, but involve the truth in their fall. For instance, if a person depreciates pleasure, and yet is once seen to make it his object, he is thought to incline to pleasure as being universally desirable, the mass of men being incapable of nice distinctions.

True statements, therefore, of such matters seem to be most expedient, not with a view to knowledge merely, but to life and conduct:

for they are believed as being in harmony with facts, and so they prevail with the wise to live in accordance with them.

But enough of such considerations : let us now proceed to the current opinions respecting pleasure.

THIS IS THE END OF THE
FIRST CHAPTER

NOW Eudoxus thought pleasure to be the chief good, because he saw all beings, both rational and irrational, striving after it: and he argued, that since in all cases that which is desirable is good, and that which is most desirable is the best, the fact of all being drawn to the same thing, proved this thing to be the best for all: 'For each,' he said, 'finds what is good for itself, just as it does its proper nourishment, and so that which is good for all, and which all strive after, is the chief good.'

His theories were accepted, not so much for their own sake, as because of his excellent moral character; for he had the highest reputation for temperance, and therefore it was not thought that he said these things because he was a lover of pleasure, but that he really was so convinced.

And he thought his position was not less proved by the argument from the opposite of pleasure; that is, since pain was in itself an object of avoidance to all, the opposite must be in like manner an object of desire.

Again he argued, that that is most desirable, which we choose, not by reason of, or with a view to, any thing further; and that pleasure is confessedly of this kind, because no one ever goes on to ask to what purpose he is pleased, feeling that pleasure is in itself desirable.

Again, that when pleasure is added to any other good, it makes it more desirable; as, for instance, to just or temperate conduct; and good can only be increased by itself.

However, this argument at least seems to prove that pleasure belongs to the class of goods, and not that it does so more than any thing else: for every good is more desirable in combination with some other, than when taken quite alone. In fact, it is by just such an argument, that Plato proves that pleasure is not the chief good: 'For,' says he, 'the life of pleasure is more desirable in combination

II. o

with prudence, than apart from it; but if the compound be better, then simple pleasure cannot be the chief good; because the chief good cannot by any addition become more desirable than it is already'; and it is obvious, that nothing else can be the chief good, which, by combination with any of the things in themselves good, becomes more desirable.

What good is there then, which is incapable of such addition, and at the same time admits of our participating in it? for that is the sort of good of which we are in search.

Those, on the other hand, who maintain that what all desire is not necessarily good, may be said to talk nonsense, for what all men think, that we say is true. And he who would cut away this ground from under us will not bring forward things more dependable; because if the argument had rested on the desires of irrational creatures, there might have been something in what he says, but since rational beings also desire pleasure, how can his objection have any weight? and it may be that, even in the lower animals, there is some natural good principle superior to themselves which aims at their proper good.

Nor does that seem to be sound which is urged respecting the argument from the opposite of pleasure : I mean, some people say, 'it does not follow that pleasure must be good because pain is evil, for evil may be opposed to evil, and both evil and good to what is indifferent'; now what they say is right enough in itself, but does not hold in the present instance. If both pleasure and pain were bad, both would have been objects of avoidance; or if neither, then neither would have been, at all events they must have fared alike : but now men do plainly avoid the one as bad, and desire the other as good, and so there is a complete opposition.

Nor again does it follow that because pleasure is not a quality, it therefore is not a good, for virtuous acts are not qualities, nor is happiness, yet surely both are goods.

Again, it is argued that the chief good is definite, but pleasure indefinite, in that it admits of degrees.

Now if they are led to this conclusion

because it is possible to be more or less pleased, then the same thing will apply to justice and all the other virtues, in respect of which clearly it is said, that men are more or less of such and such characters, according to the different virtues, for they are more just or more brave, or one may practise justice and temperance more or less.

If, on the other hand, they mean that the indefiniteness lies in the pleasures themselves, then it may be they miss the true explanation, namely, that some pleasures are unmixed and others mixed; for just as health, being in itself definite, admits of degrees, why should not pleasure do so, and yet be definite? In the former case we account for it by the fact, that there is not the same adjustment of parts in all men, nor one and the same always in the same individual: but health, though relaxed, remains up to a certain point, and differs in degrees; and of course the same may be the case with pleasure.

Again, assuming that the good is perfect and complete, while movements and processes are incomplete, the opponents of pleasure try to show that pleasure is a movement and a coming into being.

But they do not seem to be right even in saying that it is a movement: for every movement is either quick or slow, if not absolutely like that of the universe, at least relatively; but pleasure is neither quick nor slow. One may be quickly pleased, as one may be quickly angry; but the feeling of pleasure cannot be quick, even relatively, as can walking, growing, and the like.

Of course the passage to a state of pleasure may be quick or slow, but the enjoyment of pleasure, the actual being pleased, cannot be quick.

And how can pleasure be a coming into being? For it seems that it is not possible for anything to come into being out of anything, but a thing is resolved into that out of which it came. Pain, therefore, must be the dissolution of that which pleasure brings into being.

Again, they say that pain is a falling short of the natural state, and pleasure a replenishment.

But these are affections of the body. If then pleasure really is a replenishment of the natural state, that which is replenished, namely, the body, must be that which feels the pleasure. But this seems not to be the case. Pleasure, therefore, is not a replenishment, but where there is replenishment, there is pleasure, where exhaustion, pain.

This view of pleasure would seem to have been suggested by the pains and pleasures connected with natural nourishment; for, when people have felt a lack, and so have had pain first, they, of course, are pleased with the satisfaction of their want.

But this is not the case with all pleasures: those attendant on mathematical studies, for instance, have no such antecedent pain, nor among the pleasures of the senses have those of smell, nor again, many sounds, and sights, and memories, and hopes. What is there, then, of which these pleasures can be the becoming? For here there is nothing wanting which can be said to be replenished.

And, to those who object to pleasure on the ground that some pleasures are disgraceful, we may reply that these are not really pleasant; for it does not follow because they are pleasant to the ill-disposed, that we are to admit that they are pleasant except to them; just as we should not say that those things are really wholesome, or sweet, or bitter, which are so to the sick, or those objects really white which appear so to people suffering from ophthalmia.

Or we might say thus, that the pleasures are desirable, but not when derived from these sources: just as wealth is desirable, but not at the price of treachery; or health, but not at the cost of eating any food however disagreeable.

Or again, may we not say that pleasures differ in kind: those derived from noble sources, for instance, are different from those arising from disgraceful ones; and it is not possible to experience the pleasure of the just man without being just, or of the musical man without being musical; and so on of others.

The distinction commonly drawn between the friend and the flatterer, would seem to show clearly either that pleasure is not a good, or that there are different kinds of pleasure: for the former is thought to have good as the object of his intercourse, the latter, pleasure only; and this last is reproached, but the former men praise, as having different objects in his intercourse.

Again, no one would choose to live on condition of having a child's intellect all his life through, though receiving the highest possible pleasure from such objects as children receive it from; or to take pleasure in doing any of the most disgraceful things, though sure never to be pained.

There are many things also which we should endeavour to obtain, even though they brought no pleasure with them; as sight, memory, knowledge, virtue; and the fact that pleasures do naturally follow on these, makes no difference, because we should certainly choose them, even though no pleasure resulted from them.

It seems then to be plain, that pleasure is not the chief good, nor is every kind of it desirable: and that there are some desirable in themselves, differing in kind, or in their sources from those that are not desirable. Let this then suffice by way of an account of the current maxims respecting pleasure and pain.

THIS IS THE END OF THE
SECOND CHAPTER

CHAPTER III

NOW what is the nature and character of pleasure will be more plain if we entirely recommence the subject.

An act of sight is thought to be perfect or complete at any moment; that is to say, it lacks nothing, the accession of which subsequently will complete its whole nature.

Pleasure resembles sight in this respect: because it is a whole, as one may say; and it would be impossible at any moment of time to find a pleasure, whose whole nature would be completed by its lasting for a longer time. And for this reason, pleasure is not a movement; for every movement takes a certain time, and has a certain end to accomplish; for instance, the movement of house-building is only complete when the builder has produced what he intended, that

218

is, either in the whole time necessary to complete the whole design, or in a given portion. But all the subordinate movements are incomplete in the parts of the time, and are different in kind from the whole movement, and from one another: for instance, the fitting together of the stones is a movement different from that of fluting the column, and both again from the construction of the temple as a whole: but this last is complete, as lacking nothing to the result proposed; whereas that of the basement, or of the triglyph, is incomplete, because each is a movement of a part merely.

These movements, then, differ in kind, and it is impossible at any time you choose to find a movement complete in its whole nature, but, if at all, in the whole time requisite.

And so it is with the movement of walking, and all others: for if motion be a movement from one place to another place, then too are there different kinds of it, flying, walking, leaping, and such like. And not only so, but there are different kinds even in walking, for the starting-point and the goal are not the same in the whole course, as in a portion of it; nor in one part of the course as in another; nor is crossing this line the same as crossing that; for a man is not merely crossing a line, but a line in a given place, and this line is in a different place from that.

Of movement, I have discoursed exactly in another treatise. I will now therefore only say, that it seems not to be complete at any given moment; and that the many minor ones are incomplete and specifically different, if the whence and whither can be admitted as constituting different species.

Pleasure, on the other hand, is complete in its nature at any given moment. It is plain then, that pleasure and movement must be different from one another, and that pleasure belongs to the class of things whole and complete. And this might appear also from the fact that motion is impossible except in a definite time, but pleasure is not, for the pleasure of a moment is a whole.

From these considerations then it is plain, that people are not warranted in saying that pleasure is a movement or a coming into being; for these terms are not applicable to all things, but only to such as are divisible into parts, and are not wholes. We cannot speak of the coming into being of an act of sight, or of a mathematical point, or of a unit, nor is any one of these a movement or a coming into being. Neither then is there a movement or a coming into being of pleasure, for it is, as one may say, a whole.

THIS IS THE END OF THE THIRD CHAPTER

CHAPTER IV

NOW every sense exercises itself upon its own object, and exercises itself perfectly when the faculty is in a sound condition, and the object is the noblest of those that fall within its range, for the perfect exercise of a faculty seems to mean this. We may assume that it makes no difference whether we speak of the faculty itself, or of that subject in which it resides, as exercising itself; in each case the exercise is best when the faculty is in the best condition, and the object the noblest of those that fall within its scope. And this exercise of the faculty will be not only the most perfect, but also the most pleasant; for the exercise of every sense is attended with pleasure, and the same is true of every intellectual operation and speculation; and that is most pleasant which is most perfect, and that most perfect, which is the exercise of the best faculty upon the noblest of the objects that fall within its scope.

And pleasure perfects the exercise of the faculty. But pleasure does not perfect it in the same way as the faculty and object of sense do, when these are as they should be; just as health and the physician are not in the same way causes of a healthy state.

And that the exercise of every sense is attended with pleasure is evident, for we commonly say that sights and sounds are pleasant. It is plain also that this is especially the case when the faculty is best, and its object is best: and when both the sensible object and the sentient subject are such, pleasure will always exist, supposing of course an agent and patient.

Furthermore, pleasure perfects the exercise, not in the way of an inherent state, but as a superadded finish, such as is the bloom of those who are in their prime. Therefore so long as the object of thought or sense is such as it should be, and also the perceptive or contemplative subject, there will be pleasure in the exercise; for when that which has the capacity of being acted on, and that which is apt to act, are alike and similarly related, the same result follows naturally.

How is it then that no one feels pleasure continuously? It is probably because we grow weary, for no human faculty is capable of continuous exertion; and so, of course, pleasure cannot be continuous either, for it is the result of activity. But there are some things which give pleasure when new, but give less pleasure afterwards, for exactly the same reason: that at first, the mind is roused, and exercises itself on these objects with its powers at full tension; just as they who are gazing steadfastly at any thing; but afterwards the activity ceases to be so intense, and becomes careless, and so the pleasure too is dulled.

Again, a person may conclude that all men desire pleasure, because all desire life, and life is a kind of activity, and every man works at and with those things which also he best likes; the musical man, for instance, exercises his hearing upon melodies; the studious man exercises his intellect upon speculative questions, and so forth. And pleasure perfects the activities, and therefore life, which men desire. No wonder then, that they also desire pleasure, as it perfects life to each, which is itself desirable. We will take leave to omit the question whether we desire life for the sake of pleasure, or pleasure for the sake of life; for these two plainly are closely connected, and do not admit of separation; as pleasure is impossible without activity, and every activity is perfected by pleasure.

And this is one reason why pleasures are thought to differ in kind, because we suppose that things which differ in kind must be perfected by things so differing: it plainly being the case with the productions of nature and art; as animals, and trees, and pictures, and statues, and houses, and furniture; and so we suppose that, in like manner, activities which are different in kind, are perfected by things differing in kind. Now the activities of the intellect differ specifically from those of the senses, and these last from one another; therefore so do the pleasures which perfect them.

II. P

This may be shown also from the intimate connexion subsisting between each pleasure and the activity which it perfects. For the activity is increased by its proper pleasure, as if the activity is pleasant we are more likely to form a true judgment, or arrive at an accurate result in any matter. Thus, those men become geometricians who take pleasure in geometry, and they apprehend particular points more completely: in like manner men who are fond of music, or architecture, or any thing else, improve, each on his own pursuit, because they feel pleasure in it. The pleasures, then, help to increase the activity, and that which helps to increase it must be closely connected with it; but when things are specifically different, the things that are closely connected with them must also be specifically different.

Yet this may be shown even more clearly by the fact that the pleasures arising from one kind of activity are impediments to the exercise of another; for instance, people who are fond of the flute cannot keep their attention to conversation or discourse when they hear the sound of a flute; because they take more pleasure in flute-playing than in the activity they are at the time engaged on; in other words, the pleasure attendant on the flute-playing destroys the activity of conversation or discourse.

Much the same kind of thing takes place in other cases, when a person is engaged in two occupations at the same time; the pleasanter of the two thwarts the other, and, if the disparity in pleasantness be great, thwarts it more and more, till the less pleasant of the two acts is discontinued altogether.

This is the reason why, when we are very much pleased with any thing, we do nothing else, and it is only when we are but moderately pleased with one occupation, that we vary it with another: people, for instance, who eat sweetmeats in the theatre, do so most when the performance is indifferent.

Since then its proper pleasure raises the exercise of any faculty, making it both more permanent and better, while pleasure from another source injures it, it is plain that there is a wide difference between these pleasures.

In fact, pleasures which are alien to any activity have pretty much the same effect as the pains proper to it; for the pains which are proper to an activity destroy it, as when one man finds writing or calculation unpleasant and painful, he does not write, or does not calculate, as the case may be. So then, contrary effects are produced upon the activities by the pleasures and pains proper to them, by which I mean those which arise upon the activity, in itself, independently of any other circumstances. As for the pleasures alien to an activity, we have said already that they produce a similar effect to the pain proper to it; that is, they destroy the activity, only not in the same way.

Well then, as activities differ from one another in goodness and badness, some being desirable, some undesirable, and some indifferent, so it is with pleasures, as each activity has its own proper pleasure attached to it. Thus the pleasure that is proper to a good activity is good, that attached to a bad one is bad: for even the desires for what is noble are praiseworthy; and for what is base, blamable.

Furthermore, the pleasures attendant on activities are more closely connected with them, even than the desires after them; for these last are separate both in time and nature, but the pleasure coincides with the activity, and is so inseparable from it as to raise a question whether the activity and the pleasure are identical; but pleasure does not seem to be the same thing as thought or sensation; this would be absurd, but the impossibility of separating them gives some people the impression that they are the same.

As then the activities are different, so are their pleasures; now sight differs from touch in purity, and hearing and smelling from taste; therefore, in like manner, do their pleasures; and again, intellectual pleasures from these sensual, and the different kinds both of intellectual and sensual, from one another.

It is thought, moreover, that every living thing has a pleasure proper to itself, as it has a proper function; that pleasure of course which accompanies the exercise of its faculties. And the soundness of this will appear upon particular inspection; for horse, dog, and man have different pleasures; as Heraclitus says, an ass would sooner have hay than gold; in other words, provender is pleasanter to asses than gold. So then the pleasures of animals specifically different are also specifically different, but those of the same, we may reasonably suppose, are without difference.

Yet in the case of human creatures, they differ not a little: for the very same things please some, and pain others: and what are painful and hateful to some, are pleasant to, and liked by, others. This is true of sweet things; the same things will not seem sweet to the man in a fever, and to a man in good health: nor will the invalid and the person in robust health have the same notion of warmth. The same is the case with other things also.

Now in all such cases, we hold that things are what they appear to be to the virtuous man. But if this opinion is correct, as it is usually held to be, and if virtue, that is, the good man, in that he is such, is the measure of every thing, then those must be real pleasures which give him the impression of being so, and those things pleasant in which he takes pleasure. Nor is it at all astonishing, that what are to him unpleasant, should give another person the impression of being pleasant, for men are liable to many corruptions and defilements; and the things in question are not pleasant really, but only to these particular persons, and to them only as being thus disposed.

Well, of course, you may say, it is obvious that we must not assert those pleasures which are confessedly disgraceful, to be real pleasures, except to depraved tastes. But of the pleasures which are thought to be good, what kind, or which, are to be called the proper pleasures of man? It is plain from a consideration of the activities, for the pleasures follow upon these.

Whether then there be one or several activities which belong to the perfect and truly happy man, the pleasures which perfect these activities must be said to be specially and properly the pleasures of man; and all the rest in a secondary sense, and in various degrees, according as the activities are related to those highest and best ones.

THIS IS THE END OF THE
FOURTH CHAPTER

CHAPTER V

NOW that we have discussed the various forms of virtue, and friendship, and pleasure, it remains to give a sketch of happiness, since we assume happiness to be the one end of all human things: and we shall save time and trouble, by recapitulating what was stated before.

Well then, we said that it is not merely a state; because, if it were, it might belong to one who slept all his life through, and merely vegetated, or to one who fell into very great calamities. If these possibilities displease us, and if we must rather define happiness as an activity of some kind, as was said before, and if activities are of different kinds (some being necessary and desirable with a view to other things, while others are so in themselves), it is plain that we must rank happiness among those things which are desir-

able for their own sakes, and not among
those which are so with a view to something
further : because happiness has no lack of any
thing, but is self-sufficient.

By desirable in themselves, are meant those
activities from which nothing is sought beyond
the activity ; and virtuous actions are thought
to be of this kind, for to do what is noble and
excellent, is one of those things which are
desirable for their own sake alone.

And again, such amusements as are
pleasant ; for people do not choose them with
any further purpose : in fact, they receive more
harm than profit from them, neglecting their
persons and their property. Still the common
run of those who are judged happy take refuge
in such pastimes, which is the reason why those
who have varied talent in such find favour
with despots ; for they make themselves pleasant in that which the despot desires, and
what he desires is pastime.

Now these things are thought to be elements of happiness, because men in high
position devote their leisure to them : yet it
may be that such men are not a criterion : for

a high position is no guarantee of virtue or
intellect, which are the only sources of all
virtuous activities.   And if these men, never
having tasted pure and liberal pleasure, have
recourse to pleasures of the body, we are not
therefore to think these more desirable : for
children too think that those things which are
precious in their eyes are the best.

We may well believe, that as children and
men have different ideas as to what is honourable, so too have the bad, and the good :
therefore, as we have many times said, those
things are really honourable and pleasant
which seem so to the good man : and as to
each individual, that activity is most desirable,
which is in accordance with his own state, so
to the good man that is so, which is in accordance with virtue.

Happiness then does not consist in amusement ; in fact, it is absurd to suppose that the
end is amusement, and that we toil and suffer
all our life long for the sake of amusing ourselves.   For we choose every thing in the
world, so to speak, with some further end in
view, except happiness, for that is the end

comprehending all others. But to be serious, and to labour for the sake of amusement, is plainly foolish, and very childish; while to amuse one's self with a view to steady employment afterwards, as Anacharsis says, is thought to be right: for amusement is a kind of recreation, and we need recreation, for we are unable to labour continuously.

Recreation, therefore, is not an end, for it is taken with a view to activity afterwards.

Again, it is held that the happy life must be a life of virtue, and such a life is serious, and does not consist in amusement. Moreover, those things which are done in earnest, we say, are better than things merely laughable and amusing; and that the activity of the better part of man's being, or of the better man, is more serious; and the activity of the better man is at once superior, and more capable of happiness.

Then, again, as for the pleasures of the body, any ordinary person, or even a slave, might enjoy them, just as well as the best man living; but no one supposes a slave to share happiness, except so far as it is implied in life. For happiness does not consist in such pastimes, but in virtuous activities, as has also been stated before.

THIS IS THE END OF THE
FIFTH CHAPTER

IF happiness is a virtuous activity, it is reasonable to suppose that it is the activity of the highest virtue, that is to say, of the best part of our nature. Whether then this best part is reason, or something else which is thought naturally to rule and to lead and to conceive of noble and divine things, or whether it is in its own nature divine, or the most divine part of our being, the activity of this part in accordance with its own proper virtue must be the perfect happiness.

That it is a contemplative or speculative activity has been already stated: and this would seem to be consistent with what we said before, and with truth; for, in the first place, this activity is of the highest kind, as the reason is the highest of our faculties, and the subjects with which it is conversant the highest of all which fall within the range of our knowledge.

237

Next, it is also most continuous: for we are better able to contemplate, than to do any thing else whatever, continuously.

Again, we think that pleasure must be in some way an ingredient in happiness, and of all virtuous activities, the activity of wisdom, or philosophic speculation, is confessedly most pleasant: at least, philosophy is thought to possess pleasures that are admirable in purity and permanence; and it is reasonable to suppose that the time passes more pleasantly with those who possess knowledge than with those who are seeking for it.

And what is called self-sufficiency will be most of all found in the speculative activity. The actual necessaries of life, indeed, are needed alike by the wise man, and the just man, and all the other characters; but when they are sufficiently supplied with these things, the just man needs people towards whom, and in concert with whom, he may do justice; so does the temperate man, and the brave man, and so the rest; while the wise man can contemplate and speculate even when by himself, and the wiser he is, the more is he able to do so. It may perhaps be better for him to have fellow-workers in his speculations, but nevertheless he is certainly more self-sufficient than anybody else.

Again, this activity would alone seem to be desired for its own sake, as nothing results from it beyond the fact of having contemplated; whereas from all things which are objects of moral action, we do mean to get something beside the doing them, be the same more or less.

Also, happiness is thought to imply leisure; for we toil that we may have leisure, and make war in order that we may enjoy peace. Now the activity of all the practical virtues is displayed either in politics or in war, and actions of this sort are incompatible with leisure; those of war entirely, because no one chooses war, or prepares for war, for war's sake: he would indeed be thought a bloodthirsty villain, who should make enemies of his friends to secure the existence of fighting and bloodshed. The activity of the politician also is incompatible with leisure, beside the actual work of government, it seeks for power and dignities, or at least happiness for the man himself and his fellow-citizens, which is something different from politics, and is proved to be different by our search for it.

If then of all virtuous actions, those of politics and war are pre-eminent in honour and greatness, and these are incompatible with leisure, and aim at some further end, and are not desirable for their own sakes, but the activity of the reason, being apt for contemplation, is thought to excel in earnestness, and to aim at no end beyond itself, and to have its proper pleasure which helps to increase the activity; and if the attributes of self-sufficiency, and capacity of rest, and unweariedness (as far as is compatible with the infirmity of human nature), and all other attributes of the highest happiness plainly belong to this activity, this must be perfect happiness, if attaining a complete duration of life; for in happiness there must be nothing incomplete.

But such a life will be higher than mere human nature, because a man will live thus, not in so far as he is man, but in so far as there is in him a divine element: and in proportion as this divine element excels his composite nature, so far does the activity thereof excel that of any other virtue. And therefore, if reason, as compared with human nature, is divine, so too will the life in accordance with it be divine, compared with man's ordinary life.

Nevertheless, we ought not to listen to those who advise us as men to mind only human affairs, or as mortals only mortal things; but, so far as we can, we ought to make ourselves like immortals, and do all with a view to living in accordance with the highest part of our nature; for small as it may be in bulk, yet in power and preciousness it is far superior to all the others.

In fact, this part would seem to constitute each man's self, since it is supreme and above all others in goodness: it would be absurd then if a man were to prefer the life of some other being to the life which is properly his own.

And here will apply an observation made before, that whatever is proper to each is naturally best and pleasantest to him: such then is to man the life in accordance with reason, as a man's reason is in the truest sense the man. This therefore will be also the happiest life.

And the life which is in accordance with the other kind of virtue will be happy in a secondary sense, for the activities in accordance with this are proper to man: I mean, we do actions of justice, courage, and the other virtues, towards one another, in contracts, services of different kinds, and in all kinds of actions and feelings too, by observing what is befitting for each: and all these plainly are proper to man. Further, moral virtue is thought to result in some points from physical circumstances, and to be, in many points, very closely connected with the passions.

Again, prudence and moral virtue are very closely united; since the principles of prudence are in accordance with the moral virtues, and these are right when they accord with prudence.

Moral virtues, moreover, as bound up with the passions, must belong to the composite nature, and the virtues of the composite nature are proper to man : therefore, so too will be the life and happiness which is in accordance with them. But the happiness which consists in the exercise of the reason is separate and distinct : and let this suffice upon the subject, as great exactness is beyond our purpose.

This happiness would seem, moreover, to require but a small supply of external goods, or certainly less than does that happiness which is the result of moral virtue. As far as necessaries of life are concerned, we will suppose both characters to need them equally, for though, in point of fact, the politician does take more pains about his person than the philosopher ; yet the difference will not be important, but when we come to consider their activities, there will be found a great difference.

The liberal man must have money to do his liberal actions with, and the just man to meet his engagements ; for mere intentions are uncertain, and even people who are un-just make a pretence of wishing to act justly. The courageous man will need strength, if he is to perform any of the actions which appertain to his particular virtue, and the temperate man will need opportunity of temptation, else how shall he or any one of the others display his real character?

But if the question be asked, whether it is the moral purpose or the actions that have most to do with virtue, as virtue implies both: it is plain that the perfection of virtuous action requires both: but for the actions many things are required, and the greater and more numerous they are, the more. On the other hand, he who is engaged in speculation needs none of these things for his work, it may rather be said that they are hindrances to speculation; but as a human being, and living in society, he chooses to do what virtue requires, and so he will need such things for maintaining his character as man, though not as a speculative philosopher.

And that the perfect happiness must be a kind of speculative activity, may appear also from the following consideration: our conception of the gods is, that they are above all blessed and happy: now what kind of

moral actions are we to attribute to them ?
those of justice ? nay, will they not be set in
a ridiculous light if represented as forming
contracts, and restoring deposits, and so on ?
well then, shall we picture them performing
brave actions, withstanding objects of fear
and meeting dangers, because it is noble to
do so ? or liberal ones ? but to whom shall
they be giving ? and further, it is absurd to
think they have money or any thing of the
kind.   And as for temperate actions, what
can theirs be ? would it not be a degrading
praise, that they have no bad desires ?   In
short, if one followed the subject into all details, all the circumstances connected with
moral actions would appear trivial and un-
worthy of gods.

Still, every one believes that they live, and
therefore that they display activity, because
it is not supposed that they sleep their time
away like Endymion: now if from a living
being you take away action, still more if production, what remains but contemplation ?
So then the activity of the gods, eminent in
blessedness, will be one apt for contemplative

speculation: and of all human activities, that will have the greatest capacity for happiness, which is nearest akin to this.

And this is further confirmed by the fact, that the other animals do not participate in happiness, being quite incapable of any such activity.

To the gods then, all their life is blessed; and to men, in so far as there is in it some copy of such activity, but of the other animals, none is happy, because it in no way shares in contemplative speculation.

Happiness then is co-extensive with speculation, and in proportion as people have the power of speculation, so far have they also happiness, not incidentally, but in virtue of the speculation, because it is in itself precious.

**THIS IS THE END OF THE
SIXTH CHAPTER**

CHAPTER VII

S O happiness must be a kind of contemplation or speculation; but as it is man we are speaking of, he will need likewise external prosperity, because his nature is not by itself sufficient for speculation, but there must be health of body, and nourishment, and tendance of all kinds.

However, it must not be thought, because without external goods a man cannot enjoy happiness, that therefore he will require many and great goods in order to be happy: for neither self-sufficiency, nor action, consists in excess, and it is quite possible to act nobly, without being ruler of sea and land, since even with moderate means a man may act in accordance with virtue.

And this may be clearly seen, in that men in private stations are thought to act justly, not merely no less than men in high position, but even more: it will be quite enough that just so much should belong to a man as is necessary, for his life will be happy who lives in active exercise of virtue.

Solon perhaps drew a fair picture of the happy man, when he said that he was a man moderately supplied with external goods, and who has achieved the noblest deeds, as he thought, and who has lived a temperate life: for it is quite possible for a man of moderate means to act as he ought.

Anaxagoras also seems to have conceived of the happy man, not as either rich or powerful, saying that he should not wonder if he were accounted a strange man in the judgment of the multitude: for they judge by outward circumstances, of which alone they have any perception.

And thus the opinions of the wise seem to be in accordance with our account of the matter: of course such things carry some weight, but truth, in matters of moral action, is judged from facts, and from actual life, for herein rests the decision. So what we should do is to examine the preceding statements, by referring them to facts and to actual life, and when they harmonise with facts, we may accept them, when they are at variance with them, we may conceive of them as mere theories.

Now he who exercises his reason, and cultivates it, seems likely to be both in the best frame of mind, and dearest to the gods: because if, as is thought, any care is bestowed on human things by the gods, then it must be reasonable to think that they take pleasure in what is best and most akin to themselves, that is, in reason; and that they requite with kindness those who love and honour this most, as caring for what is dear to themselves, and acting rightly and nobly. And it is quite obvious that the wise man chiefly combines all these: he is therefore dearest to the gods, and it is probable that he is at the same time most happy.

Thus, then, in this way also, the wise man will be most happy.

THIS IS THE END OF THE SEVENTH CHAPTER

CHAPTER VIII

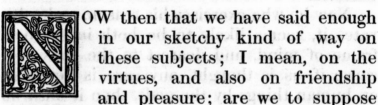

OW then that we have said enough in our sketchy kind of way on these subjects; I mean, on the virtues, and also on friendship and pleasure; are we to suppose that our original purpose is completed? Must we not rather acknowledge what is commonly said, that in practical matters mere speculation and knowledge is not the real end, but rather practice: and if so, then neither in respect of virtue is knowledge enough; we must further strive to possess and exercise it, and take whatever other means there are of becoming good.

Now if theories were of themselves sufficient to make men good, they would justly, as Theognis observes, have reaped numerous and great rewards, and it would have been our duty to provide them: but in point of fact, while they plainly have the power to guide and stimulate liberal-minded young men, and to base upon true virtuous principle any noble and truly high-minded disposition, they are as plainly powerless to guide the mass of men to virtue and goodness; because it is not their nature to be amenable to a sense of shame, but only to fear; nor to abstain from what is low and mean because it is disgraceful to do it, but because of the punishment attached to it : in fact, as they live at the beck and call of passion, they pursue their own proper pleasures and the means of securing them, and they avoid the contrary pains; but as for what is noble and truly pleasant, they have not an idea of it, inasmuch as they never tasted of it.

What mere words, then, can transform such men as these ? Surely it is either actually impossible, or a task of no mean difficulty, to change by argument what has long been engrained in the character : and it may be, it is a ground for contentment, if with all the means and appliances for goodness in our hands, we can attain to virtue.

Some ascribe the formation of a virtuous character to nature, some to habit, and some to teaching. Now nature's part, be it what it may, obviously does not rest with us; but belongs to those, who in the truest sense are fortunate, by reason of certain divine agency.

It is to be feared that reason and teaching will not avail with all; but it may be necessary for the soul of the hearer to have been previously prepared for liking and disliking as he ought; just as the soil must, to nourish the seed sown. For he that lives in obedience to passion would not listen to any advice that would dissuade him, nor comprehend it, and if this is his state, how can one reform him. In fact, generally, passion is not thought to yield to reason, but only to brute force. So then there must be, to begin with, a kind of affinity to virtue in the disposition; which must love what is noble, and hate what is disgraceful. But to get right guidance towards virtue from earliest youth is not easy, unless one is brought up under virtuous laws; for a life of temperance and endurance is not pleasant to the mass of men, and specially the young. For this reason the food, and manner of living generally, ought to be the subject of legal regulation, because things, when they have become habitual, will not be disagreeable.

Yet perhaps it is not sufficient, that men while young should get right food and tendance, but inasmuch as they will have to practise and become accustomed to certain things, even after they have attained to man's estate, we shall want laws on these points as well, and, in fine, respecting one's whole life, since the mass of men are amenable to compulsion rather than reason, and to punishment rather than to a sense of honour.

And therefore some men hold, that while legislators should employ the sense of honour to exhort and guide men to virtue, under the notion that they who have been well trained in habits will then obey; they should impose chastisement and penalties on those who disobey, and are of less promising nature ; and as for the incurable, expel them entirely : because the good man, and he who lives under a sense of honour, will be obedient ; and the baser sort, who aim at pleasure, will be kept in check, like beasts of burden, by pain. Therefore also, they say, that the pains should be such as are most contrary to the pleasures which are liked.

As has been said already, he who is to be good must have been well brought up and trained, and then live accordingly under good institutions, and never do what is low and mean, either against or with his will. Now these objects can be attained only by men living in accordance with reason, and right order, backed by force.

As for the paternal rule, it possesses neither strength, nor compulsory power, nor in fact does the rule of any one man, except he is a king, or some one in like case: but the law has power to compel, since it is a declaration proceeding from prudence and reason. And people feel enmity towards people who oppose their impulses, however rightly they may do so: the law, on the contrary, is not the object of hatred, though enforcing right rules.

The Lacedæmonian is nearly the only state in which the framer of the constitution has made any provision, it would seem, respecting the food and manner of living of the people: in most states these points are entirely neglected, and each man lives just as he likes, ruling his wife and children 'like the Cyclops.'

Of course, the best thing would be, that there should be a public system of training, and that we should be able to carry it out: but since as a public matter those points are neglected, the duty would seem to devolve upon each individual to further the cause of virtue in his own children and friends, or at least to make this his aim and purpose. Now, it would seem, from what has been said, that he will be best able to do this by making a legislator of himself; for all public systems, it is plain, are formed by the instrumentality of laws, and those are good which are formed by that of good laws. Whether they are written or unwritten laws, whether they are applied to the training of one or many, will not, it seems, make any difference, just as it does not in music, gymnastics, or any other such accomplishments, which are gained by practice.

For just as in a state, law and custom are supreme; so in a household, it is the express commands of the head, and customs; and even more, because of the ties of kinship and of obligation; for affection and obedience are naturally implanted in the members of a family.

Then, furthermore, private training has advantages over public, as in the case of the healing art: for instance, as a general rule, a man who is in a fever should keep quiet, and starve; but in a particular case, perhaps, this may not hold good; or, to take a different illustration, a teacher of boxing does not teach all his pupils to box in the same style.

It would seem, then, that the individual will be most exactly attended to under private care, because so each will be more likely to obtain what is expedient for him. Of course, whether in medicine, or gymnastics, or in any other subject, a man will treat individual cases the better for being acquainted with general rules; as, 'that so and so is good for all, or for men in such and such cases': because general laws are not only said to be, but are, the object-matter of sciences. Still, this is no reason why a person even without scientific knowledge should not be able to treat a particular case well, if he is by experience acquainted with the results of a particular kind of treatment; just as some people are thought to doctor themselves best, though they would be wholly unable to administer relief to others. Yet it may seem to be necessary, nevertheless, for one who wishes to become a real artist, and well acquainted with the theory of his profession, to have recourse to general principles, and ascertain all their capacities: for we have already stated that these are the object-matter of sciences.

If then it appears that we may become good through the instrumentality of laws, of course, whoso wishes to make men better by a system of care and training, must try to make a legislator of himself: for to treat skillfully just any one who may be put before you, is not what any ordinary person can do, but, if any one, he who has knowledge; as in the healing art, and all others which involve careful practice and skill.

Will not then our next business be to enquire from what sources, or how, one may acquire this faculty of legislation? or shall we say, that, as in similar cases, statesmen are the people to learn from, since this faculty was thought to be a part of politics ? Must we not admit that the political science plainly does not stand on a similar footing to that of other sciences and faculties ? I mean, that while in all other cases those who impart the faculties, and themselves exert them, are identical, physicians and painters, for instance ; matters of statesmanship the sophists profess to teach, but not one of them practises it, that being left to those actually engaged in it : and these might really very well be thought to do it by some singular knack, and by mere practice rather than by any intellectual process : for they neither write nor speak on these matters, though it might be more to their credit, than composing speeches for the courts or the assembly, nor again have they made statesmen of their own sons or their friends.

One can hardly suppose but that they would have done so, if they could, seeing that they could have bequeathed no more precious legacy to their state, nor would they have preferred, for themselves or their dearest friends, the possession of any faculty rather than this.

Experience, however, seems to contribute no little to its acquisition; merely breathing the atmosphere of politics would never have made statesmen of them, and therefore we may conclude, that those who would acquire a knowledge of statesmanship must have in addition, experience.

But those sophists who profess to teach statesmanship are plainly a long way off from doing so: in fact, they have no knowledge at all of its nature and objects; if they had, they would never have made it identical with, or inferior to, rhetoric: neither would they have conceived it to be 'an easy matter to legislate, by simply collecting such laws as are famous, because, of course, one could select the best,' as though the selection were not a matter of skill, and the judging aright a very great matter, as in music. For they alone, who have practical knowledge of a thing, can judge the performances rightly, or understand with what means and in what way they are accomplished, and what harmonises with what:

the unlearned must be content with being able
to discover whether the result is good or bad,
as in painting.

Now laws may be called the performances,
or tangible results of political science; how
then can a man acquire from these the faculty
of legislation, or choose the best? We do not
see men made physicians by compilations, and
yet in these treatises men endeavour to de-
scribe not only the cases, but also how they
may be cured, and the proper treatment in
each case, dividing the various bodily habits.
Well, these are thought to be useful to pro-
fessional men, but to the unprofessional, useless. In like manner it may be, that collections
of laws and constitutions would be exceedingly
useful to such as are able to speculate on them,
and judge what is good, and what is bad, and
what kind of things fit in with what others.
But those, who without this qualification should
go through such matters, cannot have right
judgment, unless they have it by instinct,
though they may become more intelligent in
such matters.

Since then those who have preceded us

have left uninvestigated the subject of legislation, it will be better perhaps for us to investigate it ourselves, and, in fact, the whole subject of politics, in order that our philosophy of human life may be completed, as far as in us lies.

First then, let us endeavour to get whatever fragments of good there may be in the statements of our predecessors; next, from the polities we have collected, ascertain what kind of things preserve or destroy states, and what particular constitutions; and the causes why some states are well and others ill managed: for after such enquiry, we shall be the better able to take a concentrated view as to what kind of constitution is best, what kind of regulations are best for each, and what laws and customs.

**THIS IS THE END OF THE
EIGHTH CHAPTER**

lies.

and customs.

THIS IS THE END OF THE
EIGHTH CHAPTER.

DATE DUE